"The golden thread of truth that is weaved throughout Debbie Cohen's I AM formula for success will empower you for life."

- Susan D. Steiner, PhD, Business Consultant, Yale University and The Wharton School

If you don't buy this book for yourself... buy it for your favorite niece or nephew, child, student, sister or brother. And if they're not old enough to read it yet, give them a copy as an investment for their future. Read it yourself and practice the exercises so you can be the best mentor in the world for them.

- *Ruth Levy, mother and mentor, Florida*

For her niece in Illinois...
My sister sent your book to my college-aged daughter. I poured through the book when I was trying to sort out my life after a 23-year marriage had ended. I am now working in a job that is double the salary that I made a year ago, finished a program in microcomputers and was nominated to the junior college honor society this spring. Yesterday, I bought my first new car, by myself, with my own credit. I thanked God, the universe and my angels for helping me to achieve all the good that I have in my life! Now I want to thank you for your inspiration, clarification and help!

- *Dianne Hillock, mother and business woman, Illinois*

This book is the next step in child psychology.

- *Becky Lookinghawk, mother and artist, Oregon*

I have completed your book and it is awesomely fantastic. Your book is the key for many who are searching and who are not sure what it is they are looking for. The concepts you have presented and the manner in which they have been presented have quieted a deep yearning within me. When we understand what it is we crave, it is safe to move forward, to take a risk.

- *Maggie Onopa, mother and friend, Wisconsin*

Reach Your Stars! helped me make some bold-faced confrontations with emotions and concerns that I had only begun to recognize. I have highlighted three key areas for personal growth and development that I intend to pursue: personal peace; the restoration of relationships, and self-acceptance. Finally, it has saved me from a destiny of writing about "the time my life almost happened to me" and encouraged me to actually start living it... and living it fully.

- *Madeleine Kuderick, mother and senior executive, Florida*

Reach Your Stars!

A guide to fulfill your dreams... not someday, but NOW!

Dear Lynn, Jeff, Samantha & Andrew

Best wishes! Dream Big + step forward, you will FLY!

Love, Debbie

★ ★ ★ ★ ★ ★ ★ ★

Reach Your Stars!

A guide to fulfill your dreams...
not someday, but NOW!

By Debbie Happy Cohen

Manufactured in the United States of America

Cohen, Debbie Happy
Reach your stars! : a coaching guide to fulfill your dreams--not someday, but now!
p. cm.
Includes bibliographical references.
LCCN 2002090171
ISBN 0-9717493-0-2

1. Success--Psychological aspects.
2. Self-actualization (Psychology) I. Title.

BF637.S8C64 2002 158.1
QBI02-200139

Edited by: Willy Mathes, Anne Miller, Connie Brown, Sue Bley
Art Director: Sue Bley
Photographer: Ellis Richman

Published by Bee Happy Publishing, imprint of Total Success Coaching, Inc.
2300 NE 196 Street, Miami, FL 33180

This book is dedicated to my sister Lisa and my brother David, and to all the children and dreamers who brighten this world.

I love you,
Debbie

"Once you know how important you are, you can reach up and touch the stars."

Debbie Happy Cohen

Also by Debbie Happy Cohen

Compact Discs

The "I AM" Formula for Success - Live Seminar with visualization exercises.

Seminars

Reach Your Stars!™ (*45-minute seminar for students of all ages*)

Total Success 101™ (*90-minute seminar for educators*)

Total Success™ (*Full-day public seminar*)

The Dream Factor: A Quality Customer Service Seminar™

The L.U.C.K.Y. Formula: Dealing with Difficult People

Before You Get a Job, Get a Life!

Mastering Positive Thinking

Transform Self-Sabotage into Success

For More Information

If you wish to contact the author, call: (813) 931-7707, or Fax: (813) 354-3540

Or write Debbie Cohen at her website: www.reachyourstars.com

Contents

Steps to Reaching *Your* Stars!

The following exercises and sections were created by Alfonso Castaneira.
Call (727) 669-6313 for further details.
Your Life Balance Triangle
Rate Your Success, Happiness and Love
The Law of Magnetism (available on audio cassette)
The Boxing Effect
The Law of Experience
The "Book of Miracles" exercises (Parts 1 and 2)
Life Map – Who Are You Becoming?

Acknowledgments

To my mentors and coaches, the people who encouraged me to live my dreams: Your voices live inside of me, and I hope to touch others as profoundly as you touched me.

To my protegé and clients, the people whose desires for a better life propelled me forward: Thank you for allowing me to guide you. Watching you blossom and grow has been the greatest feeling in the world. This book is a written answer to many of the questions you have asked.

To my family and friends who believed in my dreams: Thank you for your kindness and encouragement; you fed me when I was hungry, warmed me when I was cold, and helped me find the courage to keep going when I was afraid. Thank you for loving me. I would not be here without you!

To my success team: You are angels who have helped me give birth to the Reach Your Stars! book and program. Having you in my life has made the journey not only easier but more exciting and fulfilling. I enjoy growing and learning with you.

In the self-growth arena, it is overwhelming to think of everyone who has enhanced my life. Great ideas from many people live inside of me and have become part of me, and I am grateful for all your contributions. Reach Your Stars! would not be what it is without you. Thank you.

My love to you,
Debbie

Foreword

Sometimes in life we come upon golden opportunities without realizing it and we miss our "boat" because we didn't realize how precious the moments were of our lives.

You are holding in your hands a rare jewel. Better yet it's more like a magic lamp. It has the potential of making your deepest desires come to fruition. But, like a magic lamp, you can't just look at it, you have to do something. In the case of the lamp you have to rub it and ask for what you want. In this case you have to act. Do what this book says and magical miracles will occur.

Deb, I'm proud of you for acting and putting forth your soul in this amazing book.

May your life and every one of your readers' be full of wonder.

Your friend,
Alfonso Castaneira
A.L.F.

Alfonso Castaneira is a leader in the field of accelerated learning. He is the creator of A.L.E.R.T., an accelerated learning technology used by companies around the world to create "Learning" organizations. He is the president and founder of the Business Success Institute. You can reach Alf at Dreamgineering@yahoo.com.

Dear Reader,

Thank you for being part of my dream. It is a pleasure, a privilege and an honor to participate in yours!

A dream is like a baby; it is conceived in an instant and then it takes time to grow.

Reach Your Stars! *was conceived on November 8, 1995, the day the following letter was written. It was sent to many of my favorite authors and world leaders.*

"Each one of you has inspired me in great ways to live up to all that I am and to live my life fully by giving my gifts to the world with no inhibitions.

You are my role models, my mentors, my guides in regards to the impact I want to make in the world. Your words ring in my head when I am searching for answers.

The death of Prime Minister Yitzhak Rabin has moved me to come out of my shell and put my dreams into action. I intend to be a catalyst for world peace by uniting the forces of love on our planet, for only together will we be strong. I want to see people take action by resolving their differences peacefully, enjoying all they have in common, and making the world a safer, happier place to live."

A good book is like a stimulating conversation, and I welcome you to form your own perspectives and opinions along the way. I hope that you enjoy reading this book as much as I have enjoyed writing it for you. May the best things happen for you as you Reach Your Stars! *May your journey be filled with peace, vitality, happiness and love!*

In gratitude and love,
Debbie

Introduction

The way we see the world will determine our response to it. Problems arise when people view themselves as separate from the world: separate in time (living in the past or the future) and separate from others (feeling alone). In truth, we are deeply connected to the present and to each other. I invite you to read this book with an open mind and an open heart, that you may discover the gifts each moment brings as you awaken to the wonder in yourself and others.

This is more than a "feel good" book. Our business world and the way we make money is changing. With new technology, the jobs of the laborer are decreasing at an incredible rate. We are living in a service-oriented society, and we need people who can think clearly, build strong relationships, and make smart decisions. Businesses are seeking creative people who know their strengths and contribute them in a constructive way. Great leaders are people who are confident and able to trust themselves to follow their hearts and their visions fully; they know how to include, inspire, and serve others in order to achieve excellent results. This book is one path to developing such leaders.

Great leaders have often had great mentors. The messages you are about to read are what I wished someone would have taught me when I was 5, and then 10, and then 15, and every single year of my life after that. Life becomes so much more beautiful and easy when you know what you can and cannot control. It becomes so much richer when you know how to feel your feelings, express them, and develop relationships where everyone wins. Success in school becomes possible when you can study and retain information because you are truly interested and have a personal incentive to learn. Success in life becomes possible when you know who you are and what you value, and when you persist in that direction.

"And I think to myself, what a wonderful world."
Louis Armstrong

The exercises you are about to experience have generated clarity of direction, more effective action and more positive relationships for many people at home, school and work.

Children, I am speaking on your behalf, and I would love your feedback on my expression. I am here for you and I love you infinitely. You are our future. You are our guiding lights. I hear your call for a better way. I hear that you want your leaders to be open, inspiring and real. You want to be taught tolerance, honesty and love by example. This book is meant to light the way for you and for the people who lead you. You are our angels. Thank you!

Parents, educators, and business leaders: Thank you! By reading this book, you are affirming your openness to a better way. I will be stretching your minds, and I ask only that you continue to read and practice the exercises with YOURSELF. As you look in the mirror and transform, you will become a healthier and happier leader for the people you serve and for the children who look up to you.

Children and employees copy what we do; they do not follow what we say, unless we follow what we say. If a manager is rude to her employees, they will probably be rude to their customers. When a manager cares about the people she serves, her employees will likely care about the people they serve. When change needs to be made, it is important that we face the challenges and not deny their existence. It is time to join hands with the people we serve and admit to ourselves we sometimes don't have the solution. We must be open and willing to figure it out together.

It is up to us to see the strengths in our children and in our colleagues that they themselves don't see; it is time for us to inspire others to see and reflect back to us the strengths that we don't see in ourselves. THIS CHANGES LIVES! THESE ACTIONS HAVE SAVED LIVES! When someone comes into our lives and recognizes what's wonderful in us, it's hard not to notice it ourselves.

We have spent far too long *teaching* our children (reading, writing and arithmetic) at the EXPENSE of building healthy relationships with them. And we are PAYING the PRICE now. It is a heavy one. Children have killed each other. Employees have done the same. That is NOT natural.

Parents, educators, and business leaders:

ENJOY YOUR PEOPLE! LET THEM KNOW THAT YOU SEE GOODNESS AND WONDER IN THEM. LET THEM HELP YOU. LET THEM MAKE A POSITIVE DIFFERENCE IN YOUR LIFE. THIS WILL SHOW THEM THAT THEY MATTER, THAT THEY COUNT, THAT THEY ARE IMPORTANT!

Ray Kroc, founder of McDonald's®, is a good example of someone who helped his employees reach for the stars by encouraging them to reveal the best in themselves. When he first started out, he gave a badge that said "I am a management employee" to every employee. He made a suggestion box available to them. At that time, McDonald's® had monthly lunch specials, except for the month of March. It occurred to one of the young fellows that in March, we celebrate St. Patrick's Day. While sweeping the parking lot, he came up with the idea of adding green coloring and a mint flavor to the ice cream for a March special. To this day, in some cities, it is still a popular item!

I used to coach kids who were failing school or were about to, and the first thing I would ask them was, "What do YOU want? Do you want better grades? If you do, I can help you, but first let's get on the same page. Because if you want to fail, that's fine. I just ask that if you do choose the path of failing, that you at least have a great time doing it - it's better mental health that way!"

Most teens would look at me like I had just stepped off another planet! I was not playing the game that they were used to. I knew what I could control and what I couldn't. And I knew that I COULD NOT MAKE CHILDREN WANT SOMETHING THEY DID NOT WANT. First I had to win them over. More than 50% of these students, after only one or two sessions, would show a measurable increase in their grade point averages.

I learned to ask ask them what ***they*** wanted, and to get on their side. I learned that sincerity was essential or the bond of trust on which our relationship stood would be broken.
I learned to ask them what was in their hearts. The heart does not want to hurt anyone. The heart wants to express love, heal pain and create a beautiful life.

EACH ONE OF US IS BORN WITH A UNIQUE GIFT, SOMETHING WE CAN DO BETTER THAN ANYONE ELSE IN THE WHOLE WORLD. IT IS UP TO US TO FIND WHAT THAT IS IN OURSELVES, AND ENCOURAGE OTHERS TO FIND IT WITHIN THEMSELVES.

Every person that has brought greatness to humanity, whether he or she was an inventor, a peacemaker, or a parent, followed what was in his or her heart. It is time we all do the same. We all have it in us.

What about money, you may ask? This seems too idealistic, you may say. First of all, when someone has a strong desire in his or her heart, there are other people who need his or her gift or talent, people who are willing to pay for it - for her words, his cartoons, her landscaping ability, his inspiration, her math skills, his basketball talents.

Each person's gift can never be forced; it can only be gently brought out. Families, schools and businesses worldwide do better when each person is unfolding the gifts they uniquely possess. This cannot be forced or enforced. Our gifts must be inspired, nurtured and guided with a caring heart and an attentive eye.

What about order, you may ask? This looks like anarchy, you may say! For the heart to express itself, it must feel safe; a sense of order is essential to feeling safe. Children and employees crave order and need it, just as they crave creativity and play, as well as feelings of accomplishment. Living your truth does not create anarchy; it leads to balance.

There are so many programs already established in your community. Find out what they are and get involved in something that tickles your fancy. Bring love back into the schools and into the workplace. Make it okay to cry and to laugh and to be yourself. Reach out and hold someone's hand. Your actions may reach more people than you can possibly imagine.

Let's stand together and create a happy world, for our children and for our future - one step at a time, in this dance of life.

What a wonderful world indeed!

United We Stand

A note concerning the events of September 11, 2001:

The force of fear appears to be strong in our world and I feel sad that innocent people have died at the hands of "dream-stealers." But, just as a desperate mother finds the strength to lift a car off of her trapped child, we too have this strength...the strength of love.

In order to stand united and stay strong, we must be clear what we stand **<u>for</u>** even more than what we stand against. I believe we are **<u>for</u>** people everywhere who live their most heart-felt dreams of love and peace and guide others to do so. I see a world where the force of love prevails. Our dreams are like children. To grow strong they must be nurtured, protected and loved.

We must be brave. We are the dream-keepers of today and tomorrow.

This new world begins with you and me.

Debbie Happy Cohen

User Guide

How to Make the Most of This Book

What EXACTLY does "Reaching Your Stars" look like, sound like, and smell like to YOU? Ask your heart to guide you when you are answering the questions and doing the exercises throughout this book.

- Be SPECIFIC.
- Ask for ALL that you REALLY desire.
- Follow through with CONSISTENT action.
- Have FUN!

There are two ways to make the most out of this book:

1 The first way is to follow the book sequentially. Read the chapters and do the exercises. Use the "Total Success Habits Checklist" to build lasting, positive mental habits. Do this for 12 weeks for long-term results.

2 The second way is to use the "Birth of a Dream" chart (see page 11) to determine where you are on your path to your dream. Go to the corresponding chapter and do the exercises in that chapter only. (I highly recommend reading chapters 1, 2 and 3 to develop a strong foundation first.)

The chapters in the table of contents correspond with the steps on the "Birth of a Dream" chart and with the steps on the "Total Success Habits Checklist."

"All dreams come true if we have the courage to pursue them."
Walt Disney

Team Up!

- Form a "Dream Team" where a small group of people meet weekly or bi-weekly to reach their stars using the exercises in this book as a guide.

- Hire a coach. A coach can help you stay focused and will hold you accountable to your dreams. A coach may also have specialized knowledge in your field. The amount of time it takes to reach your stars will be significantly shortened by receiving direction from someone who has achieved what you desire. These are the reasons that ***every*** Olympian has a coach. Your dreams are equally important!

I welcome your questions and your success stories. Contact ***reachyourstars.com*** and they may may be posted on the site sharing good ideas and encouraging others along their journeys.

Journaling, Exercises & "Total Success Habits Checklist"

The exercises throughout this book are designed for the purpose of self-discovery and to help you move closer to your dreams, your passions and the life you desire.

Use this book as a journal to write your thoughts and answers for each exercise. Journaling will enrich your experience and provide you with a measuring stick. Reviewing your written thoughts will give you the opportunity to see how far you've come, and how you got there. The act of writing is magical and powerful. There have been times that I wrote down my dreams and goals on index cards and found them months or years later in a drawer with most of the ideas already achieved!

Before you start journaling, create a space for yourself that is peaceful and where you will have no interruptions. Relax in a place that brings you joy and enlivens your spirit, encouraging your truth to reveal itself: a comfortable couch, the park, the beach. One couple enjoyed doing the exercises together in an airplane.

Use the "Total Success Habits Checklist" (found on page 154) for 12 weeks to reinforce the ideas and develop lasting, positive thinking habits. Write in it daily and review it weekly, on the same day each week. A weekly review will give you the opportunity to see your progress and determine your next steps.

Reaching your stars takes time. Be patient and enjoy the journey. This is a learning and growing process. Picasso didn't learn how to paint overnight, and living the life that you most desire will take time. Consistency in your effort is the key. The "Total Success Habits Checklist" will help to keep you on track consistently and persistently.

Enjoy your journey!

"Your vision will become clear only when you can look into your own heart."

Carl Jung

"YES" & "I AM!" Formulas for Total Success

"Total Success" is having the ability and the confidence to be who you really are.

"YES" and "I AM!" are the guiding concepts of this book. They represent formulas designed to help you create "Total Success" and they contain basic principles which have been utilized by the most successful people throughout history.

The "YES" formula establishes the *context* of making dreams come true while the "I AM!" formula expresses the *way* to get there. The "YES" formula is interwoven throughout the entire book. It is the basis for all the success concepts. The "I AM!" formula can be found in the "Birth of a Dream" chart from steps 2 through 7.

Use the phrase "YES I AM!" to remember how to awaken your best self, every day!

YES a formula for building positive relationships

Y = *You are unique and special. You have gifts that no one else has, and it is up to you to share your gifts and strengths. You make a difference.*

E = *Everyone else is unique and special. They have gifts that no one else has, and it is up to you to appreciate their gifts and strengths. They make a difference.*

S = *Share your uniqueness and talents. Appreciate others.* Start Now.

I AM! a formula for reaching your dreams

Imagination = *Success begins with a dream. Your imagination is your greatest asset! Explore and decide what you really want. Infinite possibilities abound. Dream big!* (*chapters* 1, 2 &3)

Attitude = *Always believe in yourself and in your dreams. Have confidence and a can-do attitude. You can achieve whatever you believe strongly in your heart.* (*chapters* 4 & 5)

Motion = *Move forward and toward your dream, no matter what! Persistence is the key. Reach Your Stars!* (*chapters* 6 & 7)

! = *Celebrate every victory, both big and small! Sing! Dance! Let the rhythm of life move you! You are awesome!* (*chapter* 8)

The "Birth of a Dream" Chart

The "Birth of a Dream" chart is designed to help you easily guide yourself through the process of making your dreams come true. It will help you get closer to your dreams by showing you exactly where you are in the process, and will guide you to determine what is the next right step on your path.

A dream is like a tree. It starts out as a seed and grows into an adult tree containing fruit and seeds for new trees - new life. For a dream to grow, it needs constant attention and nourishment. The most beautiful dreams are ones whose seeds continue to flourish over time as gifts for future generations to enjoy. ***The most precious part of reaching for the stars is the love that is shared as people join hands, working together. The result is a more beautiful and peaceful world.***

Think of a dream that you have. How close are you to it?

Use the chart to help you figure out the answer and take the next step forward. Here"s how:

1. Read columns 1 and 2 to get the "big picture" (steps & analogy).
2. Read column 3 on the chart (main challenges/obstacles). Find the space where you are.
3. Take actions that are suggested to the right of that space (solution/action steps).
4. Read the last column's affirmations out loud. Also, write them on small sheets of paper and place them in obvious spots around your home/time planner/work environment. Re-read them often with passion and enthusiasm.
5. Read the corresponding chapter in the book and do the exercises.

"My mother taught me very early on to believe I could achieve any accomplishment I wanted to. The first was to walk without braces."

Wilma Rudolph
Olympic Gold Medalist

The Birth of a Dream

Steps The "I AM!" Formula	Analogy Birth of a Tree	Main Challenges Obstacles	Solution "I AM!" Formula Birth of a Dream
1 Prepare	Fertile Ground.	Uninspired, feel empty. No light in the eyes. A "whatever" attitude.	Connect with Self. Silent Moments. Peak state moments. Take care of your health: breathe deeply drink water, exercise eat nutritiously.
2 Explore **Imagination**	Idea to plant a seed.	"I'm bored." "I don't know what I want." Lacking hope. Burned out. Lack of vision.	***Imagination*** Brainstorm. Explore internally and externally new people places, and experiences.
3 Decide **Imagination**	Planting the seed.	"I'm tired." Chronic fatigue. "I think I know what I want, but I'm not sure." Uncertain of vision.	***Imagination*** Decide what path YOU want to take, then visualize stepping in that direction. Feeling energized about your decision.
4 Build Confidence **Attitude**	Feeding the seed water & sunshine.	"I don't know if I can do it / whether it's possible." Lack of certainty and confidence in self.	***Attitude*** Say "YES, I can!" Love yourself by focusing on your dream and acting on your decision.

A Chart for Total Success from Conception to Creation

Action Steps	*Goals of Learning/Affirmations*
Meditate. Connect with nature. Uplift your energy: sing, dance, yell, cheer all at the same time – WAHOO! Start a gratitude journal.	I feel innocent and peaceful. My mind is clear. I am open to all possibilities. I can glimpse my full potential. I am healthy and happy to be alive. I know I am deserving of the best in life. I give fully.
Spend time with people you admire, who believe in you and who can help you stay focused on your dreams – find a mentor. Play. Travel. Go somewhere new. Journal to explore your inner life.	I am free. I seize the day! I connect with my natural desire to express life in action. "Ah-ha!" moments, curiosity, delight are normal. I enjoy new experiences, exploring and discovering.
Establish your vision. Have a dream. Set your intent to do, have or be something. Focus on what you DO want, not on what you don't. What you focus your attention on grows. Resolve. Imagine. Feel it already achieved.	I know what I want. I feel inspired. I feel focused and happy. I have clear direction. I make many decisions. I feel curious about the outcome. Ideally, I feel confident about my footsteps and I also feel detached about the results.
Plan the steps you will take to have your vision come to fruition. Make it a mission. Commit to it. Set aside time – daily, weekly – to follow through on each step. Read inspiring biographies. Identify where you are heading and who you are becoming.	I feel excited, motivated, and confident. I have a strong desire to see my dream come to life. A clear mission. I know I can have it, do it, be it.

The Birth of a Dream

Steps The "I AM!" Formula	Analogy Birth of a Tree	Main Challenges Obstacles	Solution "I AM!" Formula Birth of a Dream
5 Balance **Attitude**	Protecting the seed from harm, nurturing it along.	Anger, blame, resentment. "No one cares." "People think I'm wasting my time."	**Attitude** Transform your doubts and fears by changing how you view the situation. Turn obstacles into opportunities.
6 Step Forward **Motion**	Seed takes root & grows into a sapling; continue to nurture & feed.	"What I'm doing is not working. I feel like giving up. Why should I continue this anyway?"	**Motion** Take baby steps. Model them after someone who has succeeded. Measure your progress.
7 Reach Out **Motion**	Sapling grows into a tree; nurture, feed, and prune it.	"I feel unmotivated. I know what I want and that I can do it, but I can't get myself into action."	**Motion** Take baby steps together with someone. Create a success team or partnership. Find a coach.
8 Celebrate !!!!!!!!!!!!	Tree gives fruit and seeds to eat and share; continue to nurture, feed, and prune.	"Is this all there is? I have it all. Now what? How can I give back *and* continue to serve?"	***Celebrate!*** Contribute! Coach! Include others in you dreams. Help others with *their* dreams. Create an industry to employ others & benefit the community.

A Chart for Total Success from Conception to Creation

Action Steps	*Goals of Learning/Affirmations*
When you feel negatively about something, "review" the situation. Look for the "gift" in things as they are. Focus on what is positive and leave the rest. Care for yourself and your dreams.	I have courage. I know that my fears are not real. I focus on what I *can* control: my attitude and my behaviors. I am determined. I can overcome any obstacle. I am patient, loving and compassionate.
Take realistic, consistent steps toward your dream. Find the best mentor you can, and model your habits after theirs. Chart how far you have come and where you're headed. Express gratitude for each step.	I am aligned with greatness. I take the steps necessary and follow in great footsteps. I am committed, involved, and I participate. When I fall, I get back up. I learn and balance even better next time.
Reach out, team up, ask for help, give help. *Every* Olympian has a coach. No one ever reaches the top alone. You are *not* alone. Find someone or a group to hold you *accountable*.	***I Reach For The Stars!*** I connect with growth and success. I feel empowered. I join others on the journey and keep my commitments.
Keep a gratitude journal, volunteer your time, have a party! Enjoy your success and revel in each moment. Create new dreams. Become a philanthropist or a coach. Give fully to live fully. Ask yourself "what next?" and listen to your heart for guidance.	I have discovered the fountain of youth! I create heaven on earth by bringing my dreams to life and helping others do the same. I enjoy my life. Yes! Yes! Yes! I feel truly rich!

Dreams and Goals

"I have a dream." Dr. Martin Luther King's words ring in the minds and hearts of ~~millions of~~ people as his legacy continues to grow years beyond his death. When a person's heart has something strong to share, there are other people who are waiting for it. What is in your heart is your gift to the world. Discover it, live it and give it.

Dreams give people hope and meaning, a reason to live. Goals are the steps that make them happen. Dreams are timeless, goals have timelines. Dreams without goals may go nowhere, but they can keep a person alive because they give hope. However, goals without dreams can be harmful. A person without a dream is alive but not really living. People without dreams are more likely to follow other people's ideas, whether or not the ideas are good ones. It is especially important that our youth are inspired to discover and follow their dreams. This happens in two ways: one, we live our dreams and serve as role models and two, we encourage others to live their dreams.

Dreams are bigger than you and create a sense of meaning and purpose in life. People who live their dreams have a place where they feel they "fit" in this world. Sometimes dreams do not directly touch other people, but living your dreams makes the world a better place whether you are growing a garden, dancing in your living room, or becoming a more peaceful person.

Living your dreams means being in love with life. When people are in love with life, they shine brighter in everything they do! You know you are living your dream when time flies, your eyes shine, you feel enthusiastic, and you want other people to feel the same. As you reach for your dreams, you develop character and you become stronger. As you learn to trust in life's process, your dreams will grow, the way grass grows. Naturally!

"What you are striving for is magic, not perfection."
Michael Eisner

"**Above all do no harm.**" Some dreams or the means to achieving them are destructive or hurtful. This book is designed to bring out the best in you by helping you achieve dreams and goals that are positive and beneficial.

Dreams ask the question: What if?
Goals ask the question: What next?

What's your dream? What if it were possible? What next?

Inspirational Leadership & True Freedom

Great leaders motivate and inspire people to work and play together and bring out the best in themselves and each other. This is different than forcing people to do what you want them to do.

The "***inspirational method***" of leadership has to do with people desiring to follow a leader. A leader gets 150% commitment from these people; they will maintain the culture and values of the leader, even when he or she is not around.

The "***forceful method***" of leadership has to do with manipulation (control for its own sake) and coercion. This type of leader gets less than 100% commitment from their team; they will do things differently than the leader when he or she isn't looking. Children and employees would rather follow inspirational leaders; in fact, they desire and are seeking them right now!

"*A great manager has a knack for making ballplayers think they are better than they think they are. He forces you to have a good opinion of yourself. He lets you know he believes in you. He makes you get more out of yourself. And once you learn how good you really are, you never settle for playing anything less than your very best.*"
Reggie Jackson

People want a sense of order. Order gives both a framework for success and a feeling of safety. A classroom, family, or work environment where "anything goes" is just as unhealthy as an environment where extreme control and coercion take place. The place where "anything goes" feels like a sports game – or traffic – in which there are no rules – it can be easy to get hurt, and you never know when you're winning, or how to win.

On the other hand, environments where "control for its own sake" or coercion exist can create adults who don't know how to think for themselves. In this environment, people feel highly pressured to succeed. Often, they appear as though they *are* succeeding (for instance, many anorexic girls are also excellent students). Or they become rebels – "reverse puppets" – people who need an authority figure to tell them what to do so that they can do just the opposite. This is as true for adults as it is for children. These two leadership concepts are on opposite ends of the same spectrum. Both discourage feelings of openness and trust, which are essential to any ***lasting*** success.

Inspirational leadership is motivating and strong. It is grounded in a sense of respect for oneself and others, and leads to true freedom. It leads to feelings of trust and safety, which promote openness, creativity, and love. Neuroses decrease as people become less afraid of making mistakes and more focused on taking healthy ***risks*** toward success. This book will help you develop the inspirational leader in you!

Note to School Leaders & Dream Teams

How can we fan our sparks of fire in a positive direction?

School leaders have requested techniques that can be easily taught to their students. Individuals have requested activities that can be done in a group setting.

At the end of this book, you will find a Treasure Chest of resources and group activities.

- ★ Programs and Books to Help you Reach Your Stars
- ★ Activities for Classrooms and Dream Teams
- ★ 57 Ways to Awaken a Creative Genius
- ★ "*Reach Your Stars!*" 45-minute seminar outline that teaches the "YES" and "I AM!" formulas for success in an inspiring and motivating way.

The best strategy for applying the concepts in this book in relationship to other people is based on the "I AM" formula:

Imagination: Imagine them reaching their dreams.
Attitude: Focus on the best in them.
Motion: Show them by example that reaching for the stars is worthwhile and cheer them on for their efforts. Encourage them to focus on the next right step.

"If your actions create a legacy that inspires others to dream more, learn more and become more, then, you are an excellent leader."

Dolly Parton

The Birth of Great Ideas

From silence, all great ideas are born;
From great ideas, all great actions are taken;
From great actions, new worlds are born, and all great things happen.

We are the soil in which great ideas are planted. We are the ones who choose whether to tap into those ideas or not, and whether or not we will act on those ideas. We are here to give birth to dreams. Through our dreams and hopes of a brighter future, we overcome obstacles and surpass many of our limitations.

Every Olympian understands this.
Every man, woman and child has this capacity.

More money, good grades, and greater love flow effortlessly into one's life when dreams are alive and encouraged to become manifest.

Business leaders, teachers, parents and friends: We are the midwives of the dreams of our children, of the people we lead, and of those we love. It is up to us to nurture them, teach them and give them hope and assistance to become the best they can be.

This book is one path to light the way.

"The intellect has little to do on the road to discovery. There comes a leap in consciousness and the solution comes to you and you don't know how or why."
Albert Einstein

Great and inspiring leaders throughout history have spoken of the importance of finding and nurturing inner peace and quiet to facilitate the sprouting of their ideas, visions and dreams. Through whatever means that feels right for you, identify the path to your inner silence, the limitless spring of inspiration and dreams within you. Go there on a regular basis, and bring into your activity the treasures and the peace you find there.

Notes . . .

The First Step

To give birth to your dream, choose healthy soil.

The soil is your mind where the seeds of your ideas take root and grow.

Imagine a hoe turning over the soil in your mind,

allowing oxygen to mix with the land.

Chapter 1

Prepare

Get ready to reach your stars!

Set Your Intent

When embarking on any journey it is wise to reflect upon and clarify your intent. What do you want to experience? For example, three people can visit a mountain together with totally different desires. One person may want a vigorous hike, another may want to relax and listen to the sounds of nature and the third person may want to study the trees.

What do ***you*** wish to achieve as a result of reading this book? Where are you now and where would you like to be? Spend some time contemplating and writing these answers in your journal.

Your intent is a great predictor of your behavior and therefore your results. You will have a tendency to notice what you are looking for and find more of the same. If you don't know what you're seeking, how will you know when you've found it? Most people have goals, and it is the wise person who knows how their goals serve their most meaningful dreams. An important question to ponder from a very young age and throughout your life is:

What is your unique talent or skill that you are here to discover and to share?

The benefits of answering this question are:

- Life will become more exciting and fulfilling.
- Your natural sense of curiosity and innocence will grow
- You will become more self-reliant.
- You will have more to contribute.
- Your sense of self-worth will grow.
- You will be interested in talents and gifts that others have to share.
- You will become more encouraging.
- You will be clearer about what you can control.
- You will be willing to ask for help from others who know more than you.

"And now here is my secret, a very simple secret: it is only with the heart that one can see rightly, what is essential is invisible to the eye."
Antoine de Saint-Exupéry

Life will become like "show-and-tell" and you will enjoy it much more! What are some of your intentions, dreams and desires? Write them on the following page.

Reflecting upon your intent requires a willingness to focus quietly. It can be done on a daily, weekly, monthly and yearly basis. It is a good idea to reflect on important decisions from a space of clarity that comes from stillness and silence. Practice this daily and you will see immediate and lasting improvements in your life.

Now ask yourself, in order to arrive at where you intend to be, what are you willing to do? (examples: change your behavior, give more of yourself, ask for more out of life, change your thought patterns, read, journal, risk looking foolish, take more steps, develop new habits).

Write what you think it will take.

Ahhh! Oxygen to the Brain

Relaxing your body and energizing your body both help to generate focus and clarity of mind by increasing your intake and flow of oxygen. Oxygen stimulates blood flow, heightens awareness and increases mental clarity. Both activities increase your ability to "peek" into a higher state of awareness as your mind becomes like fertile soil.

The following two exercises – one for relaxing and the other for energizing – lead to deep breathing and increased ability to focus.

Exercise 1: Relaxed State

Breathe deeply and relax your body in a happy and healthy way by:

- lighting candles
- communing with nature
- listening to peaceful music
- meditating
- journaling nonstop for twenty minutes
- becoming a "limp sock": During training, clowns are taught to relax their bodies by imagining themselves to be like a limp sock. They do this so they can fall without hurting themselves and can completely focus their energy on performing.

The benefits of relaxation:

- opens the mind
- puts you in a great place to listen, learn and be ready for new possibilities
- reduces stress-related diseases
- increases creativity, peace of mind, and better decision-making.

Relax when you need a great idea or when you are about to learn something new. Sometimes when you feel confused or unsure about your next best step, allow yourself to relax. You will make better decisions when you have a clear mind.

"Nature tops the list of potent tranquilizers and stress reducers. The mere sound of moving water has shown to lower blood pressure."

Patch Adams

Exercise 2: Energized State

Breathe deeply and joyfully with high energy that can be seen in your body movements.

- dancing
- belly-laughing
- singing joyfully
- cheering
- yelling YaHoo!
- jumping up and down
- skipping

The benefits of an energized state:

- instant motivation
- an immune system boost
- happy feelings in an instant for no good reason
- it's contagious!

Energizing your body is like starting your car. Once you get going, it's easy to keep going. Being in an "energized state" helps to reduce stress-related diseases and increases creativity, peace of mind, and the ability to make better decisions.

What does an energized state have to do with relaxation or silence?

When a person is in a high energy activity, they are not thinking as much, just acting. It is a way of turning off the "babbler" in the brain, and allows new thoughts to enter. Most of us think th same thoughts over and over. In order to reach your stars, you've got to be creative. Many creative people will change their physiology when they need inspiration. You can too! Start now! Do something silly with your body.

Yes, right now – go ahead! Have fun!

The advantage of these exercises is to get out of a negative state and into a more motivated and positive one.

Energized State:

Example 1: When a person gets depressed, their body pattern does almost the same exact thing every time. For some people – first they think of something that makes them feel bad, then their breathing gets softer, their shoulders stoop. Soon after, the TV is flipped on, and possibly sleep comes next. Others end up at the refrigerator and stare inside waiting for something happen. They are not hungry but will eat anyway. It's a downward spiral.

Solution: Recognize the pattern and do SOMETHING different as soon as awareness hits – something different, dramatic and happy with the body: no thinking, just do it. Make a rule: If the door to the fridge is opened while in that pattern, close the door immediately, put sneakers on and skip around the block three times. It's AMAZING! It's impossible to skip and be depressed at the same time. You may find yourself laughing hysterically moments after feeling down. By changing your body, you can change your mind including your emotions – instantly. The spiral becomes a positive one. Identify a behavior pattern in your life that has a negative spiral, and use either exercise (the "relaxed state" or the "energized state") to transform it into a positive one.

Relaxed State:

Example 2: One person used the breathing exercise to improve his golf game. He arrived at the course thirty minutes early and went for a walk concentrating on his breathing patterns, feeling relaxed and calm. During the round of golf, whenever he felt agitated, he concentrated on slowing his breathing pattern. Ultimately he shot a lower score than he had in almost 10 years. The other part of the story is he did not realize how well he had done until the last hole. He was so relaxed that he did not think about the score until he was almost done with the round!

Solution: Identify an activity that you enjoy and would like to perform better, and use relaxation to help you improve your skill.

Captain

There is a captain in you, a "boss" who is in charge of all the decisions you make. He or she holds the power to make the best decisions for yourself. The captain is you, and yet most people seem to live as if they are not aware of their captain. ***Your*** captain determines ***your*** intent. The best way to know your intent is to watch your feet (your actions).

Whatever is going on in your life, you have a choice. How are you choosing to behave? What attitude are you choosing to carry? Are your feet moving you in a direction that you really want to take, or do you have fights between your feet and your head? (This can create feelings of guilt, where your head faces one way, the way you know is right, but your feet walk the other way, the way you know is not right.)

For example, if you have a problem with another person, you have a million and one ways to respond to that person. Are your feet (your response) and your head (what you know to be right) going in the same direction? Is your response one that reflects the you that you are proud of, or is your response one that makes you feel bad about yourself? You can tell by how you feel. Do you feel defensive (do you justify and make excuses for your behavior)? Or can you look yourself in the mirror and feel really good about yourself, proud of who you are?

It is nearly impossible to identify your captain when there are many voices and "committees" all competing to be the leader. Like the wind, your captain can only be recognized by its effects - the "energy" you put forth and by your actions. ***This*** will become your legacy.

Your captain decides attitudes and responses to all situations. Many people are not aware of their captain and, as a result, follow other people's ideas blindly. *If you don't know what your dream is, then follow someone whose dream you do believe in. If you don't have your own vision, you are surely following someone else's.* It's okay to follow, just be conscious that you are doing so. Make your own decisions.

"Trust yourself. You know more than you think you do."
Dr. Benjamin Spock

Trust yourself.

Who decides what values are for you? YOU DO. The values you choose become your life's compass. We are so blessed to live in a free society. Your awareness of your inner captain determines how free you really are.

Think about where you are heading right now in your life.
What kind of person are you becoming?
Are you happy with your answers?

"You feel real joy in direct proportion to how connected you are to living your truth."
Oprah Winfrey

You Are a Vessel

A vessel is a craft (a ship, an airplane) that holds people. A vessel also holds liquids or something non-material. We describe vessels not only by what they are, but by what they carry. For example, a cruise ship holds different material than a battle ship.

What do you carry inside of your vessel, or your being? What you are carrying is being communicated, even when you are not speaking. Your body language and the energy people FEEL when they are around you communicates more than anything you say or do.

Similarly, you respond to what's inside of other people. If you really listen to your own body, you can tell when someone around you feels angry or happy. They may be good at hiding their feelings on the exterior, but there is a gut feeling you have. For example, with good friends, regardless of what they say, you have a good hunch about what's really going on. How is that? What is that feeling? How do you know? "Feeling" is one important way we communicate with each other.

Your best life is a natural extension of who you really are. It is important to "clean up" anything inside that you don't want in order to keep your communication clear and live your best life. If you don't acknowledge and throw out the garbage (bad attitudes, blame, resentment, self pity, etc.), your best self will be covered up. Other people will recognize it and may avoid you as a result. However, if you take the time to replace unhealthy habits and attitudes with healthy ones, your best self will shine and radiate to everyone. (*Transforming negative feelings into positive ones is discussed further in Chapter Five.*)

REFLECTION: What emotions are you holding in your "vessel," your body and in your mind right now? What kinds of feelings do you carry around with you most often? On a subtle level (or sometimes not so subtle), this is what you are communicating to others. Are you currently communicating what you most desire to share? What is the purpose of ***your*** vessel?

What do others FEEL when they are around you? There are two primary positions that reflect all feelings to different degrees. Do others feel open and safe around you, or do they feel closed off? If you really want to know, you can tell by their body language. Literally. Is their body relaxed o tense? Often, closed body language reflects feelings of fear and protection (think of closed fists an arms) while open body language reflects feelings of vulnerability and love.

The poem, "Friendly Soul," was inspired by a former employer of mine, a principal – a woman who proved to be a true blessing in my life. With a commitment to excellence and values of kindness and openness, she was able to create one of the best schools I had ever worked in. In my eyes, she was a vessel of love. Her intent was to create a school where people felt successfu and happy, and it showed in her attitude and behavior.

Friendly Soul

Like a large, welcoming tree,
you bend and sway with the wind.
And yet, like that tree,
you are sturdy and strong,
your roots planted firmly
in the ground.
Your soul is wise,
though you are young.
You know who you are,
yet you are open and accepting
to other ways and people.
A kind spirit,
compassionate and loving.
You have seen pain and hardship,
but your joy
and welcoming acceptance of life
is what makes me feel grateful
to know you.
Your presence in the world
truly makes it
a better place to be.

Communication and Feeling

In order to reach a dream, we must reach out. There are many lessons about giving and receiving along the path. It is important to have clear communication as you join hands with others. Communication takes place even when you are not speaking – in fact, your body language and your "vibe" tell more about your truth than your words do.

The ability to feel is the most powerful and keen sense that we have when we are young. Children know when something is right and when something is wrong, even when adults are trying to hide something. Most times, when a young child is going through a lot of emotional upset, the people who are closest to that child are also going through emotional upset. THE CHILDREN KNOW. In the past, children have been taught to turn off those sensors (don't cry, don't be upset, don't be angry, nothing's wrong), but we can no longer afford to do that. We must accept what we FEEL. Many children and adults are burdened now by things that they feel, yet do not know how to express in a healthy way.

"The body says what words can not."
Martha Graham

To help you understand what is meant by being a "FEELER," imagine the following scenes and FEEL the difference in your body, in your back, shoulder, neck and facial muscles. Imagine actually being there.

Use all of your senses.

- Think about entering someone's house where you do not usually feel comfortable. Imagine wanting to leave because you feel anxious or scared.
- Think about entering the home of someone by whom you feel loved. Imagine the warmth of his or her hello and then sitting down on a comfortable chair and enjoying your stay.

Notice your body's responses to the THOUGHTS of these scenes. You probably noticed changes in your body. Your breath may have deepened or quickened, your heartbeat may have slowed or accelerated, your muscles may have relaxed or tightened. Your body knows. Every cell in your body has a recorded memory of every experience you have ever had. Simply THINKING about the memory, will bring back the FEELINGS you had when you were there – UNLESS you consciously decide to change your perceptions.

Your feelings convey valuable and important messages to you, letting you know something is going on that needs your attention or needs to be expressed. Honor your feelings by paying attention to them and communicating them appropriately.

Exercise: Feeling the Power of Words

Read each word below and close your eyes after reading the word. Notice how each word makes you feel. If the word was a color, what color would it be? If the word was a sound, what sound would you hear? What does the word do to your breathing and muscles? What shape is it? Is it heavy or light? What images does the word conjure up?

Light

Dark

Brilliant

Heavy

Beautiful

Ugly

Snuggly

Terrifying

Phenomenal

Scary

Lovely

"I don't let my mouth say nothin' my heart can't stand."
Louis Armstrong

Which words make you feel closed? Which make you feel more open?

Notice how the words you think and say affect your feelings and your body. Words that make you feel closed are related to fear. When a person feels sad or depressed, their body slumps (closed). When a person feels angry, they sometimes close their fists. The body language of joy and love includes open hands and arms. Words that make you feel open are related to peace and harmony. Which do you prefer? Are you consciously choosing the environments, words and people you feel best with? The choice is up to you!

Motivation and Passion

People are motivated by two things: one is pain, the other is passion. Many child-rearing methods focus on how to get kids to do what you want them to do by punishment and reward – motivating them through pain. If they don't do something right, they get punished and, if they do, there is still the fear of what might happen if they don't. We all know this feeling. People feel this in the business world, as well. Whenever people don't feel safe, they feel stress, and stress is a leading cause of illness and accidents.

Many anti-drug and anti-smoking campaigns are based on fear and pain. "Say No To Drugs" is one example. I know many smokers and addicts who would have quit long ago had the "anti"-campaigns worked. How many people do you know who permanently alter their behavior when they are simply told to say no? Do you?

To motivate people (including yourself) through passion means really getting to appreciate them and helping them discover what their unique gifts are (not what *you* want them to be). It means letting go of the need for children or employees to "make the grade" or attain an outcome ***you*** are attached to. It means creating a space where they feel curious and delighted by their own accomplishments. It means supporting them in following their own bliss. If your workplace is not the best place for them, then it is probably better for everyone if they move toward what is.

What motivates you? Do you have passions in your life that guide you and propel you to move forward? If you can't think of any, it doesn't mean that they're not there; it means that they're hiding inside of you, just waiting to be discovered! Be patient. Be open to taking risks and making mistakes along the way. Look at what you can control and focus only on those things (your attitudes and your actions).

By living this way yourself, others will respect you and will be able to relate to you, even when you make mistakes (especially when you do!). You will become more human, more real, and it will be much easier for them to join together with you.

"The future belongs to those who believe in the beauty of their dreams."

Eleanor Roosevelt

Exercise: Discovering Your Purpose

What are some of your passions?
What makes time fly for you?
What do you love to do more than anything else?
What did you love to play with when you were little?
What makes you feel like time is standing still?
Who makes you feel like you are capable and wonderful?
Why?

In order to discover your life's purpose, it is important to explore your outer world ***and*** your inner world.

I remember searching for my life's purpose at the age of 21, giving the question many months of thought and attention. I was on the phone one evening with my sister, pondering the same question, when she emphatically stated, "Debbie, why don't you just get out there and ***do something***? If you don't like the experience when you get there, then you'll find out what you don't like and you can change your mind and use that knowledge to steer you toward what you ***do*** want. When you enjoy what you find, then you will have your question answered. You are not going to figure it out by staying home and thinking about it."

This was a major "ah-ha" moment for me and I immediately got off my seat and started to take action. I have used this story as a reminder to myself many times to get out of my head and into my life. I used the questions in this exercise to help me discover my purpose and guide my next action steps. You can too!

The Second Step

What are you hungry for?

Chapter 2

Explore

Explore your desires and imagine your future.
Believe in a world where everything is possible.

Success

If my life was a building,
  it would be built of words
and deeds.
Its strength would come
  from the truth of my words.
Its height would rise
  from the generosity of my
  deeds.
Its success would be determined
  by its usefulness to others
  for generations to come.

Chapter 2

You Are Already Successful

People hold many different definitions of success. What does success mean to you?

Think about it – you already are a success! You have succeeded in learning how to walk and how to talk. You probably learned how to ride a bike and to swim, as well. You learned how to read and comprehend and have developed an interest in building healthy, happy relationships.

Oftentimes, when speaking about success, we think about money. Money is included in the definition of success, but the way to define success is much more expansive than that. It includes a balanced life, happiness, vitality and love – all aspects of life that every human being is naturally motivated towards.

"Self trust is the first secret of success."
Ralph Waldo Emerson

Our lives right now are so filled with information that we can become distracted. Knowing what we really want, however, is key to finding our way through these distractions to lasting success.

The "I AM" formula for success (see page 9) is one that you have already used many times, whenever you have achieved success in your life. ***You imagined yourself succeeding (Imagination), you believed that you could (Attitude), and you took action (Motion). Awareness of this process allows you to apply what you already do well to create your best life.***

Recognizing this formula will shorten the time it takes to live the life you most desire.

You, like most people, know that you want to feel successful, happy, and loved; but have you ever defined what they mean to YOU?

Along your journey of reaching for your dreams, it is important that you be open to the idea that you already are worthy, wonderful, whole and complete. You do not need to chase any "ideal" in order to be successful. That would only exacerbate the idea of believing you are not enough. You do not need to do, reach or have anything in order to be and love who you are. Reach ***your*** stars to extend and expand the best in you!

Measuring Success

In sports, every game has rules and every game has measurements of some kind. You know how to measure the score, whether it's speed, number of baskets, or artistic value. You also know how to recognize a strike or a foul. Stop reading for a moment and imagine playing a sport where there are no rules and there are no measurements.

What you're probably imagining is very chaotic. In that kind of game, it can be easy to get hurt, and you never know if you're winning or not. So how do you know what to continue doing and when to stop? When there are no rules spoken, when do you begin and when do you end? How do you function as a team?

You are about to define specific aspects of life, and what they mean to you. You will define the rules of your game, and also the measurements (rating scale) in order to know how close you are to the result you desire. Be specific about your destination and where you are right now. This will help you create a focus to determine your next action steps.

Think about driving your car. By knowing where you're heading and how close you are to your destination, you can better prepare for your journey and increase the likelihood of getting there safely. Consider how often you check to see that you're driving in the center of your lane. Keeping track of your journey to your stars is just as important.

How close ***are*** you on your journey to reaching your stars?

"The person who has lived the most is not the one with the most years, but the one with the richest experience."
Jean Jacques Rousseau

The following exercises will help you define your destination and measure your progress: "Your Dream Bar," "Life Balance Triangle", and "Rate Your Success, Happiness and Love." Refer to them on a regular basis to check your course and make changes as you grow. I like to do this at least twice a year; once before the New Year and then before the fall season (when school starts), because these times of the year feel like new beginnings to me. In chapter three, you will delve more deeply into each area of your life in the Exercises "Life Map" and "Life Compass."

Exercise: Your Dream Bar

Write down the name of your favorite candy bar. If you like, go ahead and purchase one of them before you continue this exercise (for observation purposes, of course). Describe in 10 details or more, what you love about your favorite candy bar. Or, to ask the question another way, what details would you miss if they were no longer there, and would make this candy bar no longer your favorite if they were missing?

Examples: ridges in the chocolate, peanut flavor, red dots on the wrapping...

1. ____
2. ____
3. ____
4. ____
5. ____
6. ____
7. ____
8. ____
9. ____
10. ____

Did your mouth start to water when you did this exercise? If so, congratulate yourself for having a great imagination! That's exactly what you want to have happen as you describe your desires in the nextexercises. By opening your eyes to the little details that are usually taken for granted, you become more aware of (and hungry for) the benefits. Your motivation and ability to achieve your dreams increases as you become more emotionally involved in the journey.

> ***"Vision is the art of seeing things invisible."***
> Jonathan Swift

You can convert this exercise to your "dream job," "dream relationship" or any area of your life. If you are in a job, school or relationship you dislike, but it is best that you stay there for now, describe the details of what you like about the job, school or relationship. What are the benefits to staying there? ***Focus on the benefits and you will become more peaceful and happy.*** With peace in your mind, you will make better choices. You will enjoy your current experience more fully and you will move forward, closer to what you want.

Life Balance Triangle

> **"Anything the mind can conceive, it can achieve."**
> Marcus Aurelius of Ancient Rome

When I first wrote my definitions of success, happiness and love, they seemed impossible and crazy. I reminded myself that great things often start out with impossible and crazy thoughts. Electricity, the telephone, flying to the moon, E-mail, CD players, and photographs are some examples of "crazy" ideas that changed humanity for the better!

The following two exercises define the baseline to measure your progress along your journey to make your dreams real. You can review your answers every few months and update them as you change and grow.

Exercise: Your Life Balance Triangle

Write at least one page each for the following questions. Find a comfortable space where you can relax and dip into your truest thoughts and feelings,and write whatever comes to your mind.

1. ***What does success mean for you? What is your personal definition of success?***
2. ***What does happiness mean for you? What is your personal definition of happiness?***
3. ***What does it mean for you to be loved? What is your personal definition of being loved?***

Observe your ability to describe these areas of your life. Expand on your definitions until you gain as much clarity as you can.

NOTE: If you have extreme difficulty answering these questions, it may be because your desires are "blocked." Desires are natural. Yet society sometimes teaches us to suppress our desires. To describe our own definitions of success and happiness can be frightening – especially if they are different than what you were taught. Persist and stay committed to yourself. Stretch your imagination, know that ANYTHING IS POSSIBLE and BE SPECIFIC. Individual attention in addition to reading this book can be very beneficial. Take a success workshop or self-esteem seminar; hire a coach or counselor. You are worth it!

Complete this exercise before continuing.

Your personal definition of success:

Your personal definition of happiness:

Your personal definition of being loved:

Exercise: Rate Your Success, Happiness and Love

Rate each area of your life that you described in the previous section – success, happiness, and being loved – on a scale of 0 to 10. Zero means that you are experiencing none, 10 means that you are experiencing the highest heights you can dream of in that area of your life. Use your written definitions (not your current mood) to rate each area.

Rating your experience

Rating: _____
Given *your written definition* of success, how successful are you?

Rating: _____
Given *your written definition* of happiness, how happy are you?

Rating: _____
Given *your written definition* of being loved, how loved are you?

Rating your contribution

Rating: _____
Given your written definition of success, how much are you contributing to other people's success at this moment of your life?

Rating: _____
Given your written definition of happiness, how much are you contributing to other people's happiness at this moment of your life?

Rating: _____
Given your written definition of being loved, how much are you contributing to other people's feelings of being loved at this moment in your life?

Other Thoughts...

Your Ratings

Rating your experience

Read your first three ratings. What do you notice? Are they similar in number or different? The more different they are, the more out of balance your life probably feels. The more similar they are, the more balanced your life feels. The higher they are, the more satisfying your experiences are in those areas of life. Notice that your score in one life area is not dependent on the scores in other areas.

Reflection: All of the areas affect each other. What needs to change in order to find balance and satisfaction in each area? What would raising your lowest score do for your life? Some people believe that in order for one score to be high another must be low. What do you believe? Look at the beliefs that you hold. What do you want your scores to be? How will you know when you have arrived? Are your definitions specific enough to know?

Surprisingly, if you do not define your dreams and goals, you may not recognize that you have already "arrived." Your satisfaction will increase when you do.

Reread your definitions and scores on a regular basis to assess your progress and make changes as you grow.

You have what you give. As you reach your stars and increase the richness of who you are, you have more to give others. The desire to give is natural and must be honored in order to create a balanced and fulfilling life.

Rating your contribution

Interestingly, your ratings of your contribution are totally based on what you assume about other people's definitions of success, happiness and love. Do you know how your loved ones define these important areas of their life? Are you sure? When was the last time you asked?

Knowing how another person defines success, love or happiness allows you to help them experience or achieve it. Not knowing how the people in your life define success, love, or happiness leads you to make assumptions of how they experience these qualities of life.

Avoid the habit of wondering what other people are thinking, wanting or feeling. "Assuming" is 99% inaccurate and often creates a situation in which you won't succeed nor will you help others achieve love, happiness or success. It can create unhealthy expectations that lead to disappointment.

Knowing what you can control (namely, yourself) puts you in a much better position to feel satisfied with your life. Allow other people to be who they are while seeing the best in them. Your perception is your choice, their behavior is not. Get to know their uniqueness and enjoy their gifts. You will become a treasured friend for life when you do!

It is also important to express your desires and ask for what you want. This gives the people who care about you the ability to know you and love you, too. We all have a need to feel needed.

As you reach for your stars, directly ask your friends, colleagues, customers and loved ones the questions in the life balance triangle:

- What does success mean to you?
- What is your vision for our company or family?
- What makes you really happy?

By knowing what their desires are, you either will be much better equipped to help them get what they want, or decide that you are not the best person suited to meet their needs.

Everything is Possible

Congratulations! You have just planted seeds for the stars you are about to reach! Great job! This is an awesome step!

Now that you've stretched your mind and have written down what you want in your life, you are much closer to achieving it. Many studies show that people who write their goals are more likely to achieve them than those who don't.

Defining your values and desires is like deciding what kind of tree you want to grow before you plant the seed. For example, before you decide to plant a mango tree, you imagine tasting the sweetness of the mangoes when they are ripe. Before you decide to study more, first you imagine the joy of receiving an "A" or achieving your diploma. Before you ask for a raise, you imagine spending money on more things that you want or need.

"Give me a stock clerk with a goal, and I will give you a man who will make history. Give me a man without a goal and I will give you a stock clerk."

J.C. Penney

In defining and describing what you most desire, you are watering your taste buds and creating a need that will propel and compel you to fill it. Rather than having to force your will, you will move forward through inspiration and internal motivation. Your energy will increase and your abilities will heighten. This works for making more money, adjusting your body weight, becoming more loving, making friends, and winning a gold medal. You will become capable of much more than you ever dreamed!

If your desires are not clear and you're not sure of what you want: **Explore!** Get out into your community and explore new activities. Join a club, take a class, spend time in a store you never would have entered before. Then explore your inner world by tuning into your feelings. Did you enjoy your experience? Are you interested in participating again? If you do, that's great. Do it again. You can't explore too much! Have fun!

Chapter 2

Idea Explosion: Infinite Ah-Ha's!

Ideas happen when a person's experience of the outer world meets the experience of their inner world. The more new experiences we have and the more aware we are of our reactions to them, the more wonderful explosions we feel because we are discovering something new. Ah-ha!

We have thousands of examples in our history – Ben Franklin discovered electricity by observing the phenomenon (internal experience) that occurred when he flew a kite during a lightning storm (external experience). In 1960, President Kennedy knew (internal) and publicly stated that we would reach the moon in 10 years, after a scientist told him (external) that he thought "it was possible." Organizations and businesses are built around the needs of people (external) and a desire to serve (internal). "I have an idea!" happens when the internal and external world unite and ignite.

For this "fun-damental" aspect of life to grow, we must put ourselves in situations where we are experiencing newness in the external world. Here are some ideas for you to grow a healthy sense of curiosity and wonder in your life: travel, spend time in nature, visit hobby shops, read magazines outside of your usual experience, and take courses that interest you. Journal or take time to think about the experience in order to allow your own responses, opinions, feelings and ah-ha's to surface.

Having "idea explosions" on a regular basis is one of the keys to the "Fountain of Youth." Time flies and innocence is kept alive. "Ah-ha's" keep the light shining brightly in one's eyes and make an ordinary life extraordinary.

May your life's journey be filled with infinite Ah-ha's!

"Let us think of education as the means of developing our greatest abilities... in each of us there is a private hope and dream which, fulfilled, can be translated into benefit for everyone and greater strength for our nation."

John F. Kennedy

Do Something Different

When you don't know what to do, and you have been going through the same pattern over and over, do something different! Begin by asking something different of yourself first!

"The man who goes farthest is generally the one who is willing to do and dare. The sure-thing boat never gets far from shore."
Dale Carnegie

How many times have you heard people have this conversation:

"How are you?"

"Fine."

"What did you do today?"

"Nothing."

If you are bored with this conversation, DO SOMETHING DIFFERENT. Instead of asking questions, speak to that person about how YOU ARE doing, what interesting things happened during YOUR day.

This is especially true when we communicate with children. One of the biggest complaints that parents have about their children is that their kids won't talk to them or tell them what is going on. I think the kids are tired of being questioned and they want more "realness" from adults. They want to hear actual stories, real struggles and successes, and what our days are like, too. By sharing who we really are, they are more likely to do the same and share themselves with us. The level of sincerity and depth we share is usually what we get back.

Don't think they aren't listening, they are. Very closely. Our children are not robots who do what they are told. And neither are we. We won't put up with rude bosses for long, and our children won't put up with demands (even in the form of questions) for long, either.

People are amazing: they know what is real and what isn't and who is real and who isn't. In today's world, if your actions don't match your words, others will turn you off. When punished, they might behave for the moment, or shortly thereafter, but they will be doing things behind your back, and start the same negative cycle all over again.

Our children and employees are seeking inspirational leaders, people who are excited about living, who are happy with themselves, and who are healthy. It is up to us to look within and transform ourselves into inspired human beings if we are going to bring out the best in others!

Options for solutions are infinite! Search and find the solutions you are looking for!

Chapter 2

How to Ask Questions

Your questions are very revealing. You can tell much about where you are in your life and even predict some aspects of the future with a good deal of accuracy based on your current questions.

Exercise: The Importance of Asking Questions

Write three questions you have in your life right now.

____

____

____

____

____

____

____

____

____

There is a big difference between the following examples:

Person 1: Why does my child keep misbehaving?

VS.

Person 2: What can I do to encourage my child to behave appropriately?

What do you see in each of these people? Which one is more likely to find answers that are constructive and useful?

Person 1 is stuck in a box because there is no final answer to that question. It always leads to other questions, many of which do not generate change.

Person 2 believes that a solution is possible and worthy of finding and implementing.

Good questions focus on the following:

1. The present and the future.
2. What can be done.
3. On what you have control over (your own attitudes and your own behaviors).

Rather than asking, "Is my son going to graduate?" ask instead, "What can I do to inspire my son to feel confident and successful? What can I do to inspire him to want to graduate? Can I let go of my attachment to him now?" Albert Einstein and Thomas Edison were kicked out of school at young ages yet we all know their success stories! By concentrating on what you ***do*** have control over, your questions will have much more meaning.

The question "Why?" can often lead you in circles. It is a great question for stimulating a conversation or stretching your imagination, but it can get you into trouble if you use it to try to rationalize someone's behavior, or even your own.

"Why is Johnny always late?" Because he's always late. Instead, ask the question: "What can I do to change my interaction with Johnny when he's late so that we both can win?" Now that's a different story. It means looking for different answers than what you have used in the past.

Exercise: Sharpen Your Questioning Skills

Consider the questions that you wrote on the previous page. Use the clues on the following page to make them more specific, more future oriented, and more empowering. Focus on WHAT **YOU** CAN DO, and you will open the door to more and better possibilities!

Your questions, reveal an enormous amount about you including your direction. Here are a few clues to let you know where your questions are taking you.

Good questions focus on the present or future:

Past:
"Why didn't I . . ."

Present or future:
★ *"What will I . . . "*

Good questions focus on what YOU can do:

You can't control someone else's behavior:
"Why is she always late?"

You can control your own:
★ *"What can I do to keep from getting upset by her tardiness?"*

When sharing your feelings and needs - be direct:

Open-ended questions can be frustrating and can lead to resentments if the "wrong" answer is given:
"What do you want me to say?" "What are you doing later?"

It is better to state your feelings or needs clearly, confidently and respectfully:
★ *"Would you allow me to explain how I feel when you talk like that?"*
★ *"Would you stop at the store on your way home and pick up... for dinner tonight?"*

Be specific - direct questions lead to direct solutions:

Too general:
"What can I do to create a good life?" "How did I get this fat?"

More specific:
★ *"What can I do to take my career to the next level?"*
★ *"What exercise plan can I implement right now that will get me started?"*

Be self-directed:

★ *"How can I help?"*

Include others:

★ *"Would you be willing to sit down and discuss possible avenues we can take to solve this?"*

The above examples are good for taking responsibility and appropriate action. However, it is important to ask open-ended questions when you are engaging in a friendly conversation and want to encourage more dialogue. Ask questions and *feel* the answers.

★ *"Why did you move here?"*
★ *"Tell me more."*

Your Real Intention

In every story, if you are observant, you can tell from the beginning what is going to happen. For example, perhaps you've tried telling yourself, "Yes, I can do it. I know I can." But you just didn't believe it. You knew deep inside that you didn't mean it, that they were just a bunch of words – for the time being, anyway.

Maybe you were hoping the words were true, but you knew that the message wasn't going very deep. This is because of your seed thought. If you have a seed thought that you are stupid, then no matter how many times you say that you are smart, you're going to feel like you are lying and it won't work. The good news is that your seed thought is not who you are.

Get to know what your seed thought is, and then turn it around. Use the exercises, "What Your Eyes Reveal" and "Get to Know Your Deepest Thoughts" (in chapter 4) to help you discover your seed thoughts.

It is not possible for a person to be going in two directions at once. For example, a person may desire a new and better job, but if their actions are not going in that direction, then what is their real intention? The surest way to know what a person's intentions are is to watch their feet!

"As I grow older, I pay less attention to what men say. I just watch what they do."

Andrew Carnegie

Exercise: Understand the Power of Your Intent

1. Think about a major decision that you have made – get married, take a trip, or go to school. Write it down.

2. Ask yourself, "What was my seed thought, the thing that I was thinking, but may not have said when I made my decision? What was I hoping for? What was I expecting to have happen?" Write down your answers.

3. Take a look at what actually did happen. Ask yourself, "Is it possible that your originating thought influenced what came to be?

4. How determined are you to reach your stars? What is your real intention?

The Third Step

Decide which seeds to grow and plant them.

Choose wisely or foolishly, but choose.

If you don't, someone else will.

Chapter 3

Decide

Language is power. Think and speak with clarity.
Have absolute certainty that you can reach your dreams.

Chapter 3

Whatever you focus your attention on will grow.

Chapter 3

The Law of Magnetism

To the subconscious mind, the words "yes" or "no" are irrelevant. Whatever you ask it to focus on will grow and you will attract this focus into your life. It is impossible to stop thinking about what you don't want to think about.

Our words are so powerful. They create and they destroy. You have memories of what other people have said about you in the past. Some of those words stay with you for years and the feelings that come with these words may stay with you for years, too. Words have power.

How do you want your words to work for you? How do you want your words to influence others? Your words are your servants. You are playing with a life law that works. Always. Like gravity. For example, as a species, we used to think that it was impossible for us to fly. There was no way that we could defy the law of gravity. We can fly today not because we break the law of gravity, but because we work with it. It's the same thing with the law of magnetism.

For example: what "kinds" of words do you currently use? Imagine that your mind is like a computer. Input = output. The words you use come through you first and are then carbon-copied into the world.

Let's play a game to make this idea more concrete: It's time to put on your thinking cap and concentrate! Here we go:

DO NOT THINK OF EATING A PEPPERONI PIZZA.

No matter what I tell you,

DO NOT THINK OF EATING A PEPPERONI PIZZA.

DO NOT THINK OF EATING A PEPPERONI PIZZA.

What happened?

You probably thought of a pepperoni pizza, or another kind of pizza, even though I told you NOT to.

If you did not think of any pizza, read on for an explanation.

"We are what we pretend to be, so we must be careful about what we pretend to be."

Kurt Vonnegut

You cannot control your thoughts or your emotions,

but you <u>can</u> influence your thoughts and emotions

by the attitudes and actions you choose.

What Smart Advertisers Know

Your subconscious mind understands images and emotions much like a caveman or a two-year old child. It will focus on whatever you imagine, or whatever is brought to your awareness, even if you tell it not to. The most successful advertisers in the world know this. Think about how internationally well-known companies send messages to you in their commercials and billboards: (1) close-up images, (2) images that evoke emotions, and (3) repetition. These companies spend billions of dollars to reach you and their marketing executives are some of the smartest "psychologists" in the world. They know how the human mind works. It is their job to get you to change your behavior and buy their products.

What these advertisers know about your mind can be useful to you to change your own behavior. If you had a logo (one identifiable mark) to promote the best of who you are, what would that logo or mark be? Draw one! Make it a close-up image that evokes a positive feeling. Make it the best one ever! Make copies and put it in places where you will repeatedly see it.

"I know in each moment I am free to decide."

Dr. Wayne Dyer

Try the "Law of Magnetism" exercise again:

DO NOT THINK OF YOUR BREATHING RIGHT NOW.

DO NOT THINK OF YOUR BREATHING RIGHT NOW.

DO NOT THINK OF YOUR BREATHING RIGHT NOW.

What happened?

This is extremely important. It is impossible not to think of your breathing even when you are directed to not THINK OF YOUR BREATHING. (If you *were* capable of not focusing on your breathing, you were very likely concentrating on something else associated with your body).

How much energy does it take NOT to think of something? A lot! This is called suppression, and it is one of the main reasons that people commit acts of violence (more in Chapter 5). To trust yourself, you must acknowledge and be accepting of EVERYTHING that comes through you. Only then can you have the power to deal with it and make a conscious choice about it. Denial of thoughts and feelings is like denial of nuclear energy. Its power must be acknowledged, and then can it be safely redirected and transformed.

Okay, one more time. (This one is for the skeptics!)

DO NOT THINK OF THE COLOR RED.

DO NOT THINK OF THE COLOR RED.

DO NOT THINK OF THE COLOR RED.

Put your whole energy into this exercise before continuing to read.

The Boxing Effect

In the last exercise, either you thought of the color red or you may have fooled yourself into not thinking of red by probably thinking of ANOTHER COLOR! This is called "The Boxing Effect."

Even when you think you are winning the battle, the subconscious is very tricky and sets up a secondary box to keep your thoughts within the parameters that you gave it as a focus. Most people will pick ***another*** color in order not to think of red. Similarly, they may choose some other bodily function or someone else's breathing not to think of their own. Their thinking remains within a box (colors and breathing). For example, when asked to not think of the color red, few people think of the flavor of lemon juice or the feeling riding a roller coaster creates; these people would truly be using out-of-the-box thinking.

Think of some of the boxes you have created in your life by thinking about what you don't want (ie. "I don't want to be . . . fat, stressed, stupid, alone, afraid"). Name some of yours here:

____
____
____
____
____
____
____
____

"That from which you are trying to escape defines your box."
Alfonso Castaneira

The next exercise will help you get out of your boxed thinking and redirect your energy to what you most desire.

Words possess POWER!

Chapter 3

The Law of Experience

What do you really want? How easy or difficult is it for you to describe and define what you really want?

Human beings limit their experiences based on their ability or inability to describe what they are observing or what they want.

Your ability to describe what you want either limits or expands your ability to actually experience it or it can bring it to reality. I think in awe of the first people who knew that we could reach the moon. They must have "tasted" it in their minds!

Here is an effective way to expand and clarify your definition of what you want:

If you don't want X (the word you wrote on the previous page), then what you really want is the ***opposite*** of X.

For example, if you don't want "worry" then what you probably do want is peace of mind, reassurance, and tranquility.

If you want lots of money, do you tell yourself, "I DON'T WANT to be poor?" Or do you imagine spending it, investing it, and seeing it growing in your bank account?

If you want good grades, do you tell yourself, "I DON'T WANT bad grades?" Or do you imagine a wonderful report card filled with A's and B's.

"Enemies are so stimulating."
Katherine Hepburn

What you think about most is what you create in your life.

What do you think about most?

Think of a word or phrase that you think about or say that has a negative vibe to it. (For example, "I'm worried," or "That was stupid," or "I'm cursed.")

Write the negative word/phrase here: ____________________

Write three words that are the opposite of the negative word/phrase:

________________ ________________ ________________

How easy or how difficult was it for you to write the opposites? For most people, this is challenging because their vocabulary is more limited in the area of describing what they really do want. (And that's why they keep experiencing more of what they don't want!)

Re-read what you wrote in chapter two, in your definitions of success, happiness and love. Were they directed toward what you DO desire, or what you don't? You may want to edit them and make changes according to the ***Law of Experience*** now that you understand how powerful language is. Remember to:

1. State what you ***do*** want.
2. Be specific.
3. Charge your description with words that have emotional energy to you.

The next exercise will help you break down your feelings and dreams into smaller steps and clearer definitions of your deepest desires.

Exercise: "Book of Miracles" (Part I)

Write a word that has a negative tone to it that you think or say out loud.
(Choose an adjective like worried, tired, scared, or stupid.)
It can be the same or different than the previous one: _______________

Find a really good thesaurus, one that has lots of antonyms (opposites), rather than just synonyms (words that are the same). We call this a "book of miracles" because once you learn how to use it, you will create miracles in your life by attracting more of what you do want and less of what you don't. You know the saying, "Be careful what you wish for, because you just might get it!" This exercise will show you a powerful way to ask for what you want, and it also will help you interrupt your negative-thinking patterns.

Begin with a blank page.

At the top of the page, draw a circle about the size of a dime with the first letter of the negative-thinking word you want to invert (the one you wrote at the beginning of this exercise).

The reason for placing only the first letter is you introduce into the subconscious a seed of confusion (just as it would be confusing if someone simply started calling you by the first letter of your name instead of using your full name). For example, worry is no longer "worry," but "W."

From the top circle, extend three lines outward and place a circle at the end of each.

Look up the X word in the thesaurus and find three ANTONYMS. Write them in the three circles. For example, three antonyms for the word "worry" are peace of mind, reassurance, and tranquility.

Draw three lines extending outward from each of the three words with three circles at the ends of those lines.

Look up those words in the thesaurus and find three SYNONYMS for each of them.
For example, three synonyms for the word "tranquility" are serenity, calm, and peaceful; three synonyms for "peace of mind" are quiet, relaxation, and contentment; and three synonyms for "reassure" are encourage, assure, and comfort.

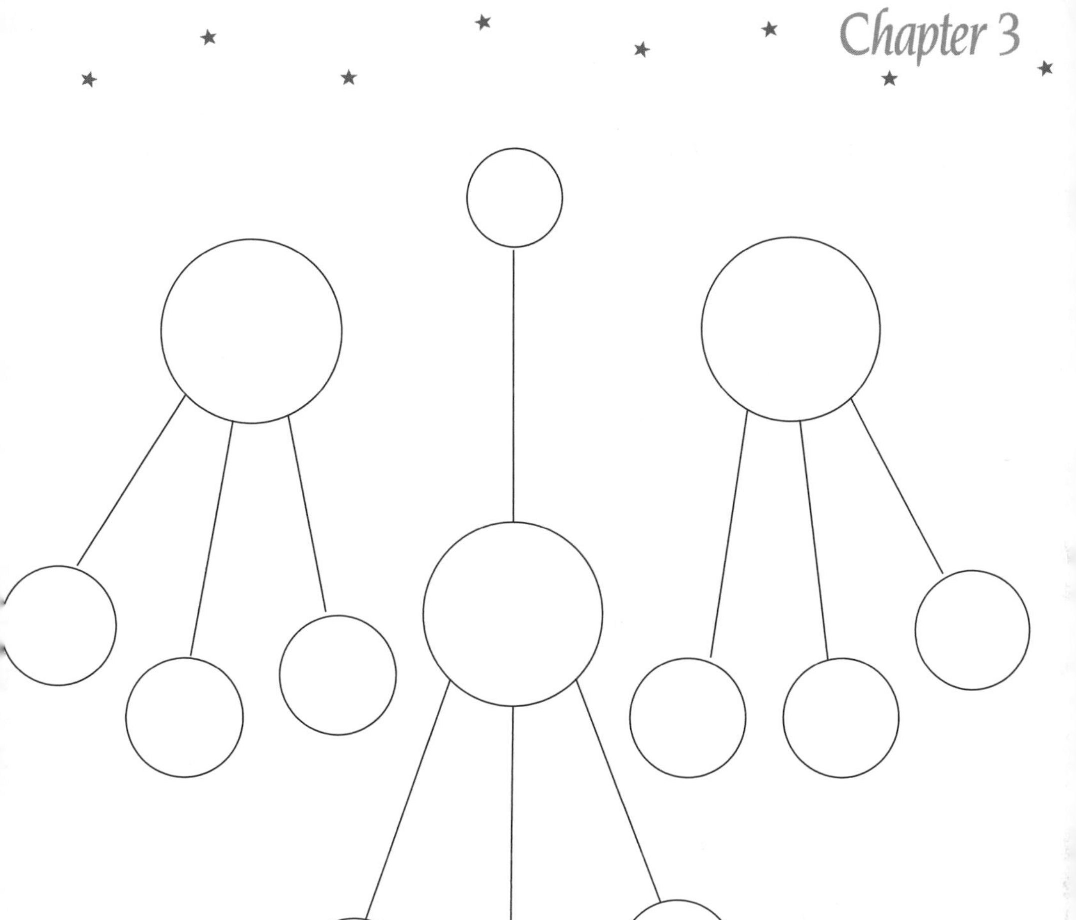

Now draw three lines extending outward from the newer words and keep seeking SYNONYMS.

Continue searching for SYNONYMS until you have exhausted your options. The purpose is to overwhelm the brain and to have a pictorial image that X is the source of everything you really do want while enriching enormously your vocabulary in the same positive direction.

After you are done, REST! Let your brain reorganize the new connections and images.

Exercise: "Book of Miracles" (Part II)

Write a personal story titled, "What do I really want?"

This story has only one requirement:
<u>You must use every single word that was found in the "Book of Miracles" exercise - part I.</u>

Complete your story before continuing to read.

By giving your mind a new point of focus, it is now able to help you experience what you really want in your life. You activate the law of experience in your favor by describing clearly what you want and feeling it.

After you write your story, ***let go***. You cannot force life to give you the specifics of everything you want. However, you can get clear about your desires and intentions. Then let go of the results and ***do the footwork***. It is important to stay open-minded and appreciate whatever happens. Too much focus on getting specific results will create rigidity which can block your awareness of newer and better opportunities. Appreciate life's mystery as your story unfolds.

Your images are now more vivid and clear, but the road to achieving them is probably unclear. Think about fairy tales and all stories of heroes . . . the dream is beautiful, but the road to getting there is never clear. That's what makes the story great; you get to see what the characters go through as they face the unknown and persevere to realize their "heroic" nature.

Your life is your story. A strong and beautiful character is built when a person maintains their ideal of what is possible and lives their life in the light of what they know to be real – even if they don't know how to get there. The fact is, taking any road in life (not just the dream-path), the road is not clear much more than a few feet. We only have so many minutes in the day and we've got to exert effort doing something, so it might as well be toward what you value most. The world is filled with infinite possibilities waiting for you!

Writing a story allows you to come up with new images and emotions for the new aspects of your life that you are creating.

Other applications of this amazing exercise:

- Apply the "Book of Miracles" exercise to several negative-thinking words.

- Expand your definitions of success, love, and happiness using your new vocabulary.

Chapter 3

Stories

Your stories reveal who you think you are. And who you think you are strongly influences your behavior and the future you are creating.

Listen to your conversations. What do they focus on? Are you the hero? Are you the victim? Do your stories include other people or are you alone in them? The stories that you tell over and over are the ones that you keep repeating in your life. Becoming aware of this can help you to change your life. All you need to do is change your stories. How do you want your stories to begin and what do you want to have happen in your stories? How do you want them to end?

"We all live in suspense, from day to day, from hour to hour; in other words, we are the hero of our story."
Mary McCarthy

Andrew Sanderbeck, author of The Power of Asking for What You Want: Jimmy's Story, took nine months to complete his book. During that time, it was amazing to watch him transform in the same way he wanted his main character, Jimmy, to transform. The more Jimmy became empowered, the more empowered my friend Andrew became. It was a truly wondrous, miraculous and life-changing experience.

Every time that I write, I am transformed as well. By putting my words down on paper, they reflect back to me like a mirror, and I am faced with asking myself if I am living what I am teaching. This is not always easy and I don't always make the change that I need to immediately, but it has helped me to grow. I have learned to celebrate my mistakes and imperfections as well as my achievements and strengths!

Dale Carnegie, who wrote the best-selling book, How to Win Friends and Influence People, was "caught" at his desk reading his own book. When questioned about this, he replied that he, too, needs a daily reminder of how to live.

Exercise: Tell Your Story (Part I)

Write a story about something you consistently share with others about yourself in your conversations. Make it one paragraph, from beginning to end. Include a title at the top of the page when you are done. Write your story in the present tense. Include details to make your story more real, and to better remember how you felt.

Complete Part I before continuing.

Exercise: What Your Story Reveals About You (Part II)

Ask yourself, "What does your story say about you?" You may want to write a few more stories or listen to yourself in conversation. The stories that you repeat the most usually have similar themes. These themes weave the tapestry of your character and your life. Answer the following questions and open your eyes to the fabric that you are creating.

Are you a participant or an observer? A victim or a villain? Do you think life is wonderful or unfair? What does your story focus on? Are you with other people or are you alone? What do you want to happen in this story? Does it go the way you want it to? Why or why not? There is a point of decision you make in every one of your stories, and you may often respond in a similar way in many of your life situations.

Are you satisfied with your storyline? If you would like the story or the ending to change, you can come up with different options regarding your own behavior or attitude ahead of time, before the situation arises again. You may want to ask a close friend or a child what they might do. Children think outside the box, so be prepared to accept their perspective. Be open to various possibilities, even if you disagree. Make a decision to feel or behave differently. This will empower you in the future to create newer and better stories.

There is one common element in every single story of your life, and that is YOU. You are the only person who you can change. I learned this when I was training my parrots to not bite or say "bad" words. What I learned was that the parrot wasn't really the one being trained, I WAS! It was me who had to realize that every time I yelled at the parrot, I was giving him the exciting attention (a great show for him!) he wanted and in order for him to tone down his behavior, I had to react much more calmly and peacefully. It was my choice. When I chose to respond consciously and quietly, the biting and yelling that my parrots displayed decreased dramatically. If I wanted the parrot not to say "bad" words, I had to keep my own language clean.

Suggestion: read stories, watch movies and listen to songs that motivate and inspire you... about myths, travelers, artists, heroes, teachers, business legends, and acts of kindness. Allow them to move you to new possibilities of what you are capable of while they raise your spirit and ignite your passion. Use them as examples of stories that you may want to tell some day.

I love autobiographies because they demonstrate how "human" successful people are. They had dreams and made mistakes just like me. They give me hope because I realize we are all human going through an adventure called life and, that if they can do it, then I can, too.

To Know a Man

To know a man's passions
Is to glimpse into his soul
And understand his world;
What drives him,
What he wants out of life,
And where he's headed.
Not to know a man's passions
Is not to truly see him
For who he is.

To know my own passions
is to know myself.

To share my passions
is my gift to the world.

Chapter 3

Time: Building Your Life's Foundation

The most precious thing in the entire world is time. It is the one thing that can never be regained. When I was about 22 years old, I had just graduated from college, and I was supposed to enter a master's degree program in counseling. The problem was, I wasn't sure that that's what I wanted. So I dropped the idea and made a decision to build a foundation for myself first, one that would last for the rest of my life.

"You may delay, but time will not."
Benjamin Franklin

For two years, I explored different jobs and practiced various arts, including poetry and drawing. I decided that I would create a life where I could look back and be glad . . . to create a lifetime of memories that would make great stories for my grandchildren. This would mean living fully. I wrote my first book of affirmations, called **I LOVE ME!**, and made a commitment to do what I loved to do for the rest of my life. I also made a commitment to touch many people's lives in a positive way.

This was far out! I knew then that I wanted to be a professional speaker and an author, but I had no idea how that would happen. Today, I am so grateful I decided to think about my values at a young age, and now I am doing what I love and inspiring others to do the same.

How well-connected do you feel to your life's foundation and to the values that are most important to you?

Success Syllabus for Life

Use the following outline to help establish your life's foundation. The "areas of life" are listed in sequential order and the ones below depend on the success of the ones above. Most of us have been taught to begin with money & grades. But truly successful people start at the beginning with a "clear mind."

1. Clear Mind A positive attitude and clear mind assures that your intentions, decisions and values will come from your best self. Always make decisions from a positive mind-frame. Your decisions become your future. A positive attitude improves your health, your relationships, your environment, career and financial status. Clear your mind and choose a positive attitude, no matter what, every day!

2. Time Only by knowing your values can you reach your stars, because you know who you are. Having clear values helps you define who you are becoming and which direction you are heading. How you spend your time affects the way you take care of your health, which relationships are most significant to you, how important your environment is, your career choices and your finances. Time is on your side when you are living your values. Regrets come from not doing the things you wish you had done. Time is ticking. Discover your values and build a life that is yours.

"There is a fountain of youth; it is your mind, your talents, the creativity you bring to your life and the lives of the people you love."

Sophia Loren

3. Health Good health allows you to participate in and enjoy the rest of the game. Having a positive attitude and valuing your body can help you stay healthy. Take care of your health. Act on youthful, age-related dreams early on (i.e. sports).

4. Relationships Relationships are the essence of life and allow you to give and receive love. All of life is built on the relationships we create, with ourselves and others. They are more precious than anything else in the world. Nurture your relationships.

5. Environment A clear environment allows you to be fully present and focused on your given activity. An inspiring setting increases your sense of peace and well being. Create an inspiring and orderly environment.

6. Vocation Your work or hobby gives you a sense of meaning and purpose. This may be the same as your dreams or it may be different. Strive to have a meaningful career or hobby that brings you joy. Serve others with excellence.

7. Money Money opens doors for worldly resources and for more options in how you spend your time. Save, spend and grow your money.

Become the most amazing and glorious person you've ever met!
Shine your light on the world!

Exercise: Life Compass - Where Are You Heading?

Reflect upon the following ideas; discuss your thoughts and feelings with a close friend if you like.

★ Where are you heading in each area of your life? Why is that desirable to you?

★ What got you started on your current journey? Is it taking you where you want to go?

★ What you want to do and where you want to go are meaningful only in the context of the following: Who do you want to be? And who do you want to become? Who you want to be and become are the basis of what you value. (These questions will be expanded on in the "Life Map" Exercise).

The amount of fun you have, how much you contribute to others and whether or not you are in harmony with your personal integrity are a reflection of how satisfied you are in those areas of life. The higher your level of fun, contribution, and integrity – the more fulfilled you will feel.

In the next exercise, you will discover what your deepest values are and create a "Code of Honor." This will increase your ability to maintain a high level of integrity with yourself in every area of your life. Your "Code of Honor" will become an easy way to always keep in mind what values are most important to you. The benefit to this exercise is that whenever you make a decision in the future, you can filter the decision through your most important values.

Exercise: Life Map - Who Are You Becoming?

Create a life map! This exercise will take a few hours and a few sittings, and will grow as you do. Create a rough draft on plain paper and then draw a larger version in color on a poster board, using a life theme that appeals to you (garden, planets, atoms, etc.).

1. On the center of your page, draw a small circle (about the size of a quarter) with rays stemming out from the circle and in the center of the circle, write your name.

2. On the end of each ray, draw a circle big enough to fit a word.

3. Write down an area of your life that is important to you in each small circle. An area of your life is something that you spend time on, or know you should or want to spend time on.

   Make your life areas specific. What kinds of things do you spend your time on and where do you wish you were spending more time? Some life areas include: health, travel, spirituality, self-care, household manager, education, intimate relationship, mentor, life mission, family, finances, friendship, wife, mother, daughter, animal lover. (One of my life areas is motherhood. I am not a mother right now, but I want to be one, so it is included on my life map.)

4. In every area of your life, you play many roles. Draw lines stemming from the small circles.

5. Draw smaller circles at the end of each of those lines and write inside them the roles you play. Writing your roles correctly is important in order to move on to the next step.

Here's how to determine your roles. Each role you play must fit correctly in the blank space:

What kind of _______________ do I want to be?

Or what kind of _______________ do I want to become?

For example, in the area of self-care, you may play the following roles: nutritionist, coach, che doctor, gardener, time manager, reader, or relaxer. Notice that many of the roles in these examples end in the letters "er."

Or perhaps in your family, you may wear many hats: mother, father, child, lover, caretaker, doctor, coach, confidant, friend, fun-sparker, party planner, movie-goer, and chef.

In your career, you may play multiple roles as well – employee, boss, friend, creator, critic, jokester, motivator, and actor.

With your finances, you may be a saver, spendthrift, investor, and philanthropist.

6. On separate sheets of paper, write each area of your life on the top of the page (the circles closer to your center circle on your life map).

On the left hand side of the page, list each role (the circles further out on your life map) you play in that area of life, and leave space underneath each role to answer the questions below.

Important: before moving on to step 7 make sure you understand and maintain integrity wi The Law of Magnetism and The Law of Experience from the beginning of this chapter. In this next exercise it is extremely important that you write ALL your statements in the positive, stating wha you DO want, not what you don't.

7. Write your answers to the questions below. The *"blank space"* is the particular ROLE you are working on. In order to create more heartfelt answers, imagine yourself at your funeral, invisible to the people who are in attendance. All the people from every area of your life are there. Imagine all the wonderful and ideal things they are saying about you. This will reveal the values that are most important to you.

Answer these questions:

What kind of _______________ do I want to be?

And what kind of _______________ do I want to become?

The difference between the two questions is who you want to be relates to the near future, and who you want to become relates to the far future.

For example, in the area of ***Intimacy***, these are some of the questions I answered about the roles I play:

What kind of LOVER do I want to be?
What kind of LOVER do I want to become?
What kind of DANCE PARTNER do I want to be?
What kind of DANCE PARTNER do I want to become?

(I have about 10 roles that I play in each of the areas of my life.)

In the area of ***Life Mission***, I answered these questions:
What kind of SPEAKER do I want to be?
What kind of SPEAKER do I want to become?
What kind of CHEERLEADER do I want to be?
What kind of CHEERLEADER do I want to become?
What kind of AUTHOR do I want to be?
What kind of AUTHOR do I want to become?

Here are some examples of how I answered questions about **Friendship**.

What kind of FRIEND *do* I *want to* BE?
Supportive, honest, reliable, spontaneous, kind, caring, open, innocent, and encouraging.

What kind of FRIEND *do* I *want to* BECOME?
Accepting, *only* loving, true to my Self, easy, leisurely, and more playful.

Take your time and listen to your heart.

You may find yourself repeating words and phrases, which is fine. You'll discover themes in step 10 when you create your "Code of Honor" and be empowered to act with greater clarity.

Before you continue, review everything you wrote and make sure that it has integrity with the "Law of Magnetism" and "The Law of Experience." Be sure that everything is written in the positiv and, if not, correct it.

8. Once you have completed step 7, gather all the pages containing your life areas and th roles you play, along with two highlighter markers of different colors.

Create a comfortable, intimate space for yourself. Play calming music or go outside if it is peaceful. Enter a quiet space in your mind and relax yourself as you enter the following scenario: Imagine a boat floating in the center of an ocean. You are on this boat, sitting on the edge, weari diving gear and you are about to dive into this ocean in search of pearls - your pearls, the deepes and most important values to you. Each pearl represents a value and each value is a jewel.

Take note of your surroundings: the gentle rocking of the boat, the warmth of the sun, the smell of the water; how you feel - calm, excited, anxious. How does your scuba gear feel? Can you hear yourself breathing? Use all your senses.

When you're ready, jump into the water. Feel the sensations both inside and outside your body. What is the temperature of the water? How buoyant are you? What else do you notice?

Now release the air from your jacket, and feel your weights taking you deeper and deeper. Slowly. Just before you reach the bottom of the ocean floor, you notice many oyster shells with pearls in them, open and waiting for you. You swim over to each pearl and move your hands over each one, without touching.

You notice that your hands slow down when you are attracted to a certain pearls, but move quickly over the ones that are not as appealing to you.

9. Now that you are in a relaxed state of mind, open your eyes gently and look at your page with your list of roles and descriptions of who you are now and who you will become.

Pick up one of your highlighters and imagine that each of your descriptions is a pearl. Highlight those pearls (descriptions) that you feel more attracted to – those which you resonate. You may remove the debris from each pearl and place it back in its shell.

When you have highlighted your "pearls" in all your life areas, using your other highlighter, go back to the beginning of the first page, and repeat the process. But this time, imagine yourself moving your hands only over those pearls that attracted you, that resonated with you (which you highlighted).

Notice how each pearl feels to you and IF IT RESONATES BACK WITH YOU. If it does, then IT IS A TRUE GEM. You may take this pearl with you. Highlight these descriptions in your new color highlighter.

Give yourself a pat on the back. Good job!

10. Now you will create your "Code of Honor." Review your pages and examine your gems. Write a list of your gems, the words that were underlined twice, and most often. These words are a reflection of your current and deepest values, the ones you will want to keep for life.

If you find you have more than 10 gems, look for the most common themes, and shorten your list based on the most important values. Imagine stringing them together like a pearl necklace.

Write this list on a business card size piece of paper and keep it in your wallet. Review it often.

Remember - what you focus your attention on will grow!

The Fourth Step

Nurture your dreams with water and sunshine.

Chapter 4

Build Confidence

Your attitude determines your latitude.

I Love Me!

I LOVE ME is important because you get what you give! If you give love, you feel love move through you. If you give anger, you get the original, they get the carbon copy! So – when you know who you are (love), then you can give and keep giving. What better way is there to become happy with yourself? And when you're happy with yourself, it's contagious. Be loving with yourself, and it will be easy for others to love you!

The next exercise will help you discover any blocks you have for loving yourself. Listening to your inner feelings is so important, because it is how you stay in touch with yourself. Many people who ignore their feelings have anxiety or stress and don't know why or how to stop it. Continued stress is the cause of many modern diseases. Staying in touch with what you are feeling will help you experience your pain, especially when it is small, so you can face it and heal it before it gets out of hand. For this reason, the benefits of the next two exercises are immeasurable!

"Love yourself first and everything else falls into line. You really have to love yourself in order to get anything done in this world."
Lucille Ball

Exercise: What Your Eyes Reveal

Your eyes are the window to your soul. Affirm that which you desire.
Look into your eyes in the mirror and affirm I AM AWESOME!. Say it at least 12 times.

What thoughts or feelings come up for you? Write them down.

Keep repeating this affirmation: I AM AWESOME!. What comes to mind as you continue repeating it? What are your inner voices saying? Are they saying, "Wow, I am wonderful, I am beautiful, and I am unique and magnificent"? Or are they saying, "This is crazy, this is for sissies"? What feelings do your thoughts trigger? Are your thoughts and feelings in harmony or in conflict?

This exercise is a great way to get to know what your deepest thoughts about yourself. It's where your obstacles in life are hidden. The river runs deep. Your deepest thoughts – not the superficial ones – are creating your current experience.

My friend Willy Mathes says it so well, "If we show our children (and all people) that who they are is worthy of care, love and respect, then they will exhibit those traits in their self-image and how they treat others."

Exercise: Get to Know Your Deepest Thoughts

Here's a really powerful exercise to get to know your deepest thoughts and release any obstacles that might be blocking you.

Fold a sheet of paper in half and number from 1 to 25 on the left side. Next to number 1, write your affirmation I LOVE ME. What is your first inner response? Write that on the right side. Do this at least a dozen times and continue until you get consistent positive or neutral responses from yourself.

Notice which emotions arise as you move through this exercise. If you get surprising answers that don't feel comfortable, be gentle with yourself. If you find your inner voices are really negative, perhaps getting extra support from a counselor or friend could help release the pain.

Remember, the greatest gift you have to give to any situation in your life is YOU! But how can you give "you" if you don't know "you?" How can you attract that which you truly desire if you're not in communication with the REAL YOU? To be authentic is the surest way to increase love in your life, because the people who will be attracted to you will appreciate the REAL YOU!

I Know That I Make a Difference

In the process of making your dreams come true, your light will begin to shine brighter and your love will grow stronger. You will feel a natural desire to share that love with others and it is important that you do so. Reaching out to make a difference in another person's life is one of the most fulfilling and satisfying things that a person can do.

Mike is a really fascinating man, who has worked with teenage runaways for 18 years. I know from my past experience in the counseling field that very few people last that long working with runaways. Most hit burnout within five or six years, tops! I asked him why he thought that was the case. He told me that most of them don't love themselves.

Now, Mike did not exactly fit the picture I had in my mind of someone who "loves himself." He was dressed in worn-out sneakers and jeans. He was wearing a comfortable beard and he had a pack of cigarettes in his back pocket. I asked him, "Mike, what do you mean by loving yourself?" His reply was the last thing I ever expected. He said, "I know that I make a difference."

This exercise will help you recognize ***your*** impact on others.

"Who you are makes a difference."
Helice Bridges

Exercise: How You Make a Difference

Write three things you do that make other people feel important, special, or uplifted. (For example: smile, listen, give sincere compliments, etc.) Describe the results you see or have seen in people whose lives you've touched by your actions.

Chapter 4

Read and Think Like a Champion

The most successful people are never-ending learners. To create the most success for yourself and the world, enjoy your own journey and educate a younger person along the way.

The next few sections contain exercises that professional athletes and successful executives use to achieve winning results. It also contains a exercise to help you increase your reading comprehension. The ideas in this chapter changed my life. They have helped me and many others to get better grades while cutting study time in half. You can relax about school, become more creative, relate better to others, achieve higher scores in sports, and find greater peace within.

It is well known we use less than 10% of our mind's ability. Get ready to use more of your brain in a smarter way. You will learn how to focus and how to move forward into the life of your dreams, no matter what you may encounter.

Successful people constantly and consistently move step by step toward their dreams. They do not allow the critical voice to get in the way of what they want. When the voice comes up, their vision is so clear that they keep moving forward anyway. This is very powerful, and it is why it's important to make sure you have set goals that come from your heart. If you really want something, it will be easier to persist when the going gets tough.

"If one advances confidently in the direction of his dreams, and endeavors to live the life which he has imagined, he will meet with a success unexpected in common hours."
Henry David Thoreau

Bryant Johnson, a two-time handball Olympian, said the turning point that determined his success was when he decided to put his dream first and not let anything else distract him. He spent his time wisely by making everything else in his life relate back to his ONE goal. The hardest part was saying "no" to some of the things he enjoyed doing – like talking to his mom on the phone when a nap was more important.

What you think about most is what you create in your life.

What do you think about most?

Exercise: Make Reading Fun!

To enjoy reading and increase your comprehension, GET CURIOUS! After my friend and colleague Alf presented this exercise, one woman who had attended his class recently saw him, ran up to him, and thanked him generously. She excitedly told him that she went from reading one book a month to three!

This exercise works best with topics you know something about. Pick a book that has a table of contents, an index, and a dust jacket.

"*The more I wonder . . . the more I love.*"
Alice Walker

1. Write a question about the book.
2. Examine the cover.
3. Read about the author.
4. Write another question.
5. Closely read the table of contents.
6. Write another question.
7. Converse with the author, argue with him or her in your mind.
8. Form an opinion.
9. Write another question.
10. Notice patterns in the index. You'll find which topics are mentioned most often, and the main bulk of information contained in the book.
11. Flip through the book quickly and highlight the areas of interest to you; especially the pictures, tables, and graphs.

Write at least five questions about the book you are reading now.

Your curiosity will keep your interest peaked as you continue through the book, and your high interest will help you retain more information. Do not read the book in order. Read the highlights and the content that interest you first. Then, later, when you read what surrounds it, you will be more interested. Ask a lot of questions as you read the table of contents. These questions should relate to the topic.

Here are a few sample questions to give you an idea of what this exercise entails. I've picked the topic "Birth of a Dream" from the table of contents of *Reach Your Stars!*.

- I wonder what giving birth has to do with a dream?
- Is this book just for women?
- Where do dreams come from?
- I wonder if everyone has dreams?
- Does my dog dream?
- How have dreams influenced my life?
- Is a big dream better than a little idea?
- Do big dreams come with fudge and walnuts?

Some people prefer to listen to information rather than to read it with their eyes. Many books are narrated on tape. You also can record a tape of the things you need to know and then listen to the information. Visit your local library for a wonderful selection of books on tape.

Ask an Expert

SAY YES to what you really want in each area of your life. Take a look at your "Exercise: Life Map" from Chapter 3. You play so many roles in your life that it is nearly impossible to know what is best for you in each one of those roles. Creating financial stability requires a different set of skills than creating a healthy, vibrant body.

If you are not an expert in a certain area of life, how do you know what is best? How do you know what to focus on and what to imagine? How do you know what baby steps to take to get there? Find an expert!

Read! Read! Read! Ask! Ask! Ask!

- ★ Read excellent financial books.
- ★ Ask money experts for financial help.
- ★ Attend seminars on subjects you're interested in.
- ★ Read excellent books on health and nutrition.
- ★ Ask a nutritionist for help in achieving a maximum feeling of wellness.

One of the best things I ever did was seek advice from alternative medicine practitioners. I now know how to increase my energy by changing my diet. I can get rid of a cold in less than a day and I can make my back feel wonderful without a massage.

"A problem well-stated is a problem half-solved."
Charles Kettering

There are so many experts in the world and we are so blessed to have them available to us in so many ways. Books, phone calls, letters, E-mail. REACH OUT! The professionals want to serve you! That's why they are in business – they're following their dreams and successfully helping others! REACH OUT to them!

Book List

Here is a list of my favorite books that have influenced my life. These "experts" have helped me ı many areas of my life. Each book helped me to imagine and achieve better life habits.

hicken Soup for the Soul: Stories to Open the Heart and Rekindle the Spirit (Book 1),
y Jack Canfield and Mark Victor Hansen
his book is a tremendous source of positive energy to me and my audiences. It is filled with short tories and poems that inspire, teach, and stimulate positive thinking. Storytelling is the oldest orm of relaying a message, and I believe it is still the most powerful.

hink and Grow Rich *by* Napoleon Hill
fter spending 20 years doing research and interviewing the most successful and influential people ı the world, Mr. Hill wrote his book in the 1930s. The book *still* flies off the bookstore shelves. The rinciples expressed are eternal and practical. Most of them have nothing to do with money, but ne ability to create success. A more recent compilation of his ideas with more modern examples ; titled ***Keys to Success.***

xcuse Me, Your Life is Waiting *by Lynn Grabhorn*
xperience the power of your feelings and learn how to direct them to achieve more of what ou want and less of what you don't. The process is easy to learn. Read the *entire* book for naximum effect.

he Learning Revolution *by Gorden Dryden and Jeanette Vos,* Ed.D.
his is the best book on learning I have ever read. Their leading-edge methods for learning at work, chool and home will change your life.

IME MANAGEMENT

he 7 Habits of Highly Effective People, The 7 Habits of Highly Effective Families , and ***irst Things First*** *by Stephen* R. *Covey*
earn how to make the most out of your time by prioritizing wisely. Time is the most precious thing ou have. The story of the "rocks in the jar" in ***First Things First*** will change your life!

HEALTH

Ageless Body, Timeless Mind *by Dr. Deepak Choprah*
I love Dr. Choprah's influence of Eastern medicine on our culture. He writes about the healing power of watching acts of kindness and love. His stories are amazing and memorable. They will stretch your mind as to the infinite possibilities of achieving wellness.

Fit For Life *by Harvey and Marilyn Diamond*
This book was the end of dieting and the beginning of vitality for me. It is easy to read, makes practical suggestions and works immediately.

Love, Medicine and Miracles *by Dr. Bernie Siegel*
Learn about the power of relaxation on the body, and how this simple exercise has actually helped reduce the symptoms in cancer patients.

Healing Back Pain *by Dr. John Sarno*
I have used this book by a friend's recommendation to get rid of back pain instantly! It worked for her after her back surgery, so I decided to try it. It *does* work!

RELATIONSHIPS

The Bridge Across Forever, One, and **Running From Safety** *by Richard Bach*
These three books span over 30 years in time, and chronicle a true love story, between Richard and Leslie-Parrish Bach. The books changed my life, enabling me to imagine a real life relationship with my soul mate. Thank you Richard and Leslie, for being my Love Mentors!

FRIENDSHIPS

Any book by SARK
Go on a journey with SARK in one of her colorful, journal-style books. She is a living example of creativity in action, with all her flaws and all her passions. This woman is *alive* and *vivacious*!

Any book or tape by Leo Buscaglia
Leo Buscaglia, also known as "Dr. Hug" wrote many, many stories of what love looks and feels like but he refused to ever try to define it. He was the first professor to develop and teach a university course called Love 101. His book Living, Loving and Learning on tape is a personal favorite.

CAREER

The Artist's Way at Work *by Mark Bryan with Julia Cameron and Catherine Allen*
When I give this book as an assignment to someone I am coaching, I always hear raving reviews and unending thanks! I regularly use their suggestions to tap into my creativity, release negative energy, and make better decisions.

What Color Is Your Parachute? *By Richard Nelson Bolles*

I Could Do Anything If I Only Knew What It Was *by Barbara Sher*
Both are helpful in discovering your passion in finding or creating the work you love.

LEADERSHIP

Synchronicity: The Inner Path of Leadership *by Joseph Jaworski*
The impact this book has had in my life is indescribable. It discusses leading-edge leadership – how it could be and must be if our world is to survive. It relates "servant leadership" and the path to getting there. It's a WOW!

FINANCES

The Richest Man in Babylon *by George Carson*
I think every human being who uses money would be wise to learn the lessons in this book: How to master and grow money to serve you for the rest of your life. Learn how money affects every area of your life and, how by viewing it smartly, you'll be better able to make it work for you.

Rich Dad, Poor Dad *by Robert Kyosaki*
This practical and easy-to-read book helped me make sense of the different kinds of possible investments, and guided me to those best for me. ***The Cash Flow Game*** is a supplement to the book and offers a real-life experience of getting out of the rat race and into your dream life.

There are many, many more experts in this world than we can imagine. Don't feel that ***you*** must know everything to survive. We are here to learn from each other.

Beta, Alpha, Theta, Delta

We have four types of brain waves: *beta*, *alpha*, *theta* and *delta*. Understanding them will help when you practice relaxed alertness. For an excellent technique, read The Silva Method and take the course (see Treasure Chest for details). For the best research findings read The Learning Revolution.

We will focus on two of these brain waves: beta and alpha. Going to alpha consciously is the key to effective learning.

When you are awake, alert and in the midst of activity, your brain waves are moving at a high speed, called *beta*. At this stage, your brain is like a sponge that is full and will not accept new information easily.

When you are sleepy (just getting out of bed or just falling asleep), your brain waves are slower; this state is *alpha*. When you relax your body and mind, your brain waves enter the *alpha* state. During that time of relaxation, your mind is like a sponge that has been squeezed dry. It is more open to believing whatever you feed it. It is prepared to receive.

During sleep or deep hypnosis, your brain wave state is in *theta*. And during deep sleep, the state is *delta*.

If you study for an exam while alert and relaxed (*alpha*) you will remember more than if you study when your mind is full and busy (*beta*).

When you daydream, your brain waves are likely in *alpha*. Relax your mind and your body the next time you take in new information and you will be able to do so much more easily. You can also use the *alpha* state of mind to help you create the life you want. Place photos and images of what you would like to create in your life next to your bed. You can see them while you are naturally in *alpha* – when you first wake up, and when you fall asleep.

Do you know what the most successful people in the world had in common as children? Surprisingly, it was not their socioeconomic background, their level of confidence, their grades or whom their parents knew.

Have you guessed? They were ***daydreamers***!

The point is - ***relax!***

Chapter 4

"The real key to effective learning can be summed up in two words: relaxed alertness."

The Learning Revolution *by* Gordon Dryden *and* Jeannette Vos

Dolphins and Whales

There are some valuable lessons you can apply to yourself by observing how dolphins and whales are taught to jump out of the water and fly through the air to do tricks. They are taught one step at a time.

Dolphins and whales learn to fly high up in the air and to touch a ball first by starting at the bottom of the pool. A brightly colored rope is placed on the bottom of the pool. Every time the dolphin swims over the rope, he gets a fish. If he doesn't swim over it, he doesn't get a fish. When he's done this a few times in a row, the rope is raised, but only about a foot. Again, if the dolphin swims over the rope, he gets a fish; if he doesn't swim over it, he doesn't get a fish. The rope is then raised higher until the dolphin is able to swim under it, but he only gets a fish when he swims over it. This process continues until the rope is raised into the air, higher and higher, until it reaches the point where the trainer decides to stop.

The "fish" (reward) that you give yourself every time you reach for your stars can be simple and fun. You can give yourself a self-high five, enjoy an ice cream cone or hot bath, even make yourself or someone else laugh! Celebrate the steps that make up your journey!

The learning and growing process can be FUN! If you ***choose*** to see it as FUN you will be more likely to continue learning, succeeding, and desiring to learn and succeed more, FLYING higher and higher!

Fly! Soar! Reach your stars!

"One can never consent to creep when one feels the impulse to soar."

Helen Keller

Chapter 4

Frustration is Fantastic!

Frustration is fantastic! It is a sign that you are in the process of learning! Frustration and being overwhelmed are judgments that most adults place on experiences when they don't catch on or complete an activity quickly enough. When the experience is judged as negative, a common reaction is to stay away from it. The price paid is a decreased ability to learn and to succeed.

Small children are the fastest learners in the human race and they learn while having fun! They are constantly in the process of experimenting: how to walk, speak, sit in a chair, put puzzle pieces in the right spaces, write, open jars, sing, build, etc. An adult might judge the experience of learning so many activities at once as overwhelming, but young children don't!

"All children are born geniuses."
Buckminister Fuller

When you were very young, you learned a lot in a relatively short amount of time; you did not judge frustration as bad. You just kept on going and doing whatever it took to figure something out. Your attention was all over the place, and you didn't try to focus on one thing all of the time. You took it all in. You would go back to figure it out when you were ready to. In The Everyday Genius, Peter Kline states: "Emblazon these words on your mind as the most important ones in this book: Learning is most effective when it's fun."

The only way to reach a dream is through experimentation and learning! It's a dream because it's never been done before. Be patient with yourself as you journey forward, and have fun!

Say YES!

Remember, you can only experience that which your mind can describe and define. It is impossible to experience anything else at all!

One way to create new experiences for yourself is to continue to repeat the same mistakes over and over again, until you've reached your threshold of pain, and are desperately seeking a new way out. Many people learn this way, but it's not the most pleasant way to learn.

A close friend of mine did just that for awhile. She said that she wanted to go out and have fun during her spare time, but instead she kept watching TV, and complained that she was feeling bored with her life. I asked her to focus on the fun that she wanted to have.

"YES!"

Yoko Ono

She wrote a list of fun things she wanted to do, and then did them. For a few weeks, the woman was absolutely glowing; she was doing things that she had always dreamed of – like going to a circus.

A few weeks later, she told me that she was feeling bored and bad about herself again. This time TV wasn't the problem. She had replaced the TV with spending time with a friend . . . all the time! She told me that she was feeling "on the fence" because she didn't want to give up the friendship. She kept talking about how she didn't want to hurt her friend. We humans are so funny; we walk around the same block over and over again, and wonder how we got to the same spot!

She forgot that as long as she was focused on leaving her friend or staying with her friend, she was still not focused on the enjoyable experiences that she was desiring.

She repositioned herself by writing a list of 20 things that she really wanted to experience. She then created timelines for at least two of those things to be done within two weeks. She was back to feeling great again! Today, she sings in a band and performs on weekends! And she rocks!

Exercise: Say Yes!

What do you want to SAY YES to in your life, but have been denying yourself? (Excuses, justifications, or negotiations are not acceptable here!) Write a list of 20 things to which you want to SAY YES! Then take action!

The Fifth Step

Remove the weeds.

Chapter 5

Balance

Stay motivated no matter what!
Negative emotions can fuel positive desires.
Transform self-sabotage into success by accepting all emotions and redirecting them toward your dream.

Chapter 5

Suppressed Energy

Where does suppressed energy go? When a person is told, "Don't lose control," and learns to hold in his feelings, the energy has to go somewhere. Sometimes it manifests actively such as ulcers and heart disease. Sometimes it manifests itself in more passive ways by never letting oneself succeed, living in "almost-land." Suppressed energy can manifest into committing violence or lying in a river of depression.

Unconsciously suppressed energy leads to self-destruction. It is so important to be conscious of our energy (which I believe is more powerful than nuclear energy). Without this awareness, it is like playing with a knife or fire without realizing their impact. Because we are discussing something that is not physical, we may not see the blood or feel the burn, but the effects do show up. Our news reports verify that.

People hurt themselves without realizing it. What emotions and experiences are being hidden underneath the veil of perfectionism in a straight "A" student – one who is "good" in every area of his or her life? How many straight "A" girls suffer from anorexia? What about "successful" doctors and dentists who have committed suicide? ***This is why it is so important for each individual to define success, clarify his or her personal values and fully accept him or her self.***

When someone really listens to us, a space is created for something new to exist. One of my favorite business leaders and bestselling author, Harvey McCay, recommends that supervisors take the time to individually listen to each one of their employees on a regular basis. In his business, employees stay on board for an average of 15 years. In today's times, that is impressive!

"It is better to be whole than to be good."
Carl Jung

Courses like "Redirect Your Life" also are extremely beneficial (see the "Treasure Chest" – the last section of this book for more information) to help people accept, release and positively direct their emotions to create closeness and feelings of emotional safety. This is new territory for us as a society and well worth the time spent and risks taken. Relationships grow stronger and deeper as a result.

Chapter 5

Self-Sabotage

1. We are energy. The atoms that make up our physical being are mostly made of space. We use our bodies to channel our energy.

2. We have free will. We can choose our attitude at any given time in any given circumstance. We can choose to make the best out of something or to make the worst out of it.

3. If we are not conscious of our energy, we may fear our own free will and protect ourselves by sabotaging our own success.

Self-sabotage is when we keep ourselves from the success that we most desire. It is a way of keeping our power under wraps and protecting ourselves from potentially getting hurt. If you take too high a step, the slide down can be much more humiliating and much more hurtful than if you stay where you are.

Self-sabotage is a way of acting powerful in hidden, unconscious ways when we are too afraid to say, "I own my power." Many of us think of that as being good.

It begins when we are children, when we are taught that it's not okay to feel certain things. "Don't be angry." "Don't be scared." "Don't cry." "Be good." When we are born, we have an infinite number of doors (experiences and feelings) available to us. As we get older, we become socialized to believe certain feelings are okay and others are bad. "Be good" means "Don't feel that," even though you DO feel it.

Thus begins the ***denial of self***.

"When dealing with people, remember you are not dealing with creatures of logic, but creatures of emotion."

Dale Carnegie

Exercise: Transform Negative Feelings

When feeling upset, follow these steps:

1. Acknowledge the feeling.
2. Accept it. Like any pain, it is there to give you a message to help you pay attention to where healing or action is needed.
3. If you are at work or in class or if it is an inappropriate setting, wait for a good time to deal openly with it.
4. Identify the need to express your feelings directly to someone, or, if it is better, work it out on your own. You may want to share it with someone you trust and somewhere safe. Don't hold back anything. Ask this person to listen and not judge anything that you say. All of it is okay no matter how he or she responds.
5. Ask what the lesson or message might be – find the treasure or the silver lining.
6. Know that everyone is doing their very best, including yourself.
7. Create a positive solution that will bring you closer to what you really want, and act on it. (chapters 1, 2, and 3).

Resentment is like taking poison and hoping the other person will die. Let it go.

All feelings are natural - neither good or bad. Problems occur when people turn the volume up too high or express the wrong feeling at the wrong time. Problems also occur when people pretend their feelings don't exist. Don't judge your feelings; accept them.

"Love is letting go of fear."
Dr. Gerald Jampolsky

Chapter 5

You Are Capable of Anything

How do you become aware of suppressed emotions if you are not conscious of them?

Your emotional power is as sharp and as dangerous as a knife. It can be used to create as well as destroy. We each have a control mechanism in ourselves that protects us from harm. Sometimes this defense mechanism can be self-sabotaging. Our fear of the unknown can actually keep us from achieving success unintentionally. We may fear that success will put more stress on our lives or our families. Or perhaps we have seen others become "different" people when they reached a certain status in their lives. This is why it is vital to put love first in everything we do. It is so essential to acknowledge our feelings and accept them.

"Enlightenment is not imagining figures of light but making the darkness conscious..."
Carl Jung

Often we suppress emotions that we think are "bad" or "unacceptable." You cannot control your thoughts or feelings, but you ***can*** free yourself from judging (and then suppressing) them.

Be aware that you are capable of feeling and thinking anything. Face whatever comes up for you. Awareness allows you to be in a more empowered position to make a better decision.

Suppressed emotion has a tendency to come out sideways after all, we are made of energy, and energy must go somewhere. That is why most people tell the same stories over and over, only changing the characters. By being conscious of what is inside ourselves, we ***can*** choose a better way.

Once, I was truly angry at someone and entertained thoughts of hurting him. In fact, I really wanted to punch him in the stomach. At first, this image surprised me! How could I even think such a thing? I began judging myself and getting angry at myself for feeling such strong anger. I thought, "How could I feel this way? I'm supposed to be a loving and kind person! Who will ever want to be close to me? I'm supposed to be nice! If only 'they' knew what I was thinking, 'they'd' think I'm terrible!"

The more I beat myself up, the angrier and more hurtful I felt. I tried to control my thoughts, but the more I did, the worse and more dramatic they became. I began to feel scared of my own emotions. I felt like my own worst enemy. I began to avoid this person and would not return any of his attempts to communicate with me. This continued for a few weeks, until I began to feel totally out of control.

Finally, I couldn't take it any longer. I decided to ***choose*** a different path. I chose to accept my thoughts and feelings the way a mother would accept a 2-year-old child who was having a nightmare – with kindness and love. No matter what thoughts or feelings crossed my mind, I would accept them and love them. They were mine.

Though I wanted a better way, I had no idea how to achieve it. I had to open my mind to new possibilities. At first my images became more violent, but I continued to accept them, knowing that I would never act on them. I asked myself what I would like to do about the situation. I received no answers in the beginning, but I continued to accept all my feelings. It took patience, but within a few days, feelings of care and love toward this person began to emerge alongside my feelings of anger. I knew I would be seeing him soon. I decided to continue and allow the thoughts of love to come through me whenever I thought of him.

When I finally saw this person, it felt like there was a huge wall between us. We talked for a while, then something started to shift. My anger started to transform into compassion. I felt forgiving. I knew our relationship would not go back to what it used to be, and I knew this was okay. I felt comfortable with myself and more safe with him. I realized if I was in his shoes and saw life from his perspective, I probably would have behaved the same way he did.

I am glad I chose to accept all my feelings and emotions. That was the key to opening my mind and allowing new possibilities to enter. I was trapped in a box of negativity as long as I suppressed the feelings that were "scary, bad, or wrong." Now I am free. Today, I have more compassion for people who feel rage and who feel out of control, because I know what it is like to feel that way, too.

Who Are You Pointing At?

Another important clue is to watch your pointer finger. Look out for the times that you blame others or get angry at others for what they say or do. When you feel anger or blame, your "buttons" are being pushed. Salt only hurts on the skin if there is an open wound. The only time someone can push your buttons is when you are capable of doing what he or she is doing, yet aren't owning up to it. Once you "own it," you can be really free to choose your reaction.

For example, many years ago, I had a really big argument with a good friend. I don't even remember what it was about, but I sure do remember how I felt. I was so mad at him! It felt awful!

I was reading a self-help book at the time and the author suggested writing a letter to my friend and expressing all the things that I was thinking and feeling about him, without sending it. When I finished, I was to take the letter over to the mirror, and read it out loud facing myself, as if it was written to me.

"Dear Debbie," I began, "You are the most ____________________ human being in the world!"
I began to laugh! My anger seemed to vanish into thin air as I realized that I too, could be all of the things I was judging my friend to be. Not only that, but the qualities he held that pushed my buttons reflected areas in my life that I needed to strengthen.

Suddenly, I felt closer to my friend and, since then, I have never been able to criticize him with the same intensity as that day. I felt more compassion for him, which began to replace the anger. I was happy that I could laugh at myself. The finger I was pointing was truly a lesson, especially when I really got the message that three fingers were pointing right back at me!

"The weak can never forgive. Forgiveness is the attribute of the strong."
Mahatma Gandhi

Reflection: What are some of your "hot buttons?" What triggers them? Who do you find yourself pointing your fingers at? What does that say about you? What would you rather feel? Focus on that new feeling and let it grow.

Chapter 5

Own All of Your Feelings

The next eye-opening exercise, based on the previous examples, has been one of the greatest keys to my success in working with children. It is hard to be angry with someone when you realize that he or she are your mirror and your teacher. This realization gave me great patience, and to be open-minded with children. I must allow them the space to speak and be heard. Then, and only then, do they listen to what I have to say.

We all live within a range of feelings. But none of the feelings are either always bad or always good. To an extent, all emotions can be appropriate in the right place and time. Taken to an extreme, these same emotions that are strengths can be harmful.

For example, one of my strengths is persistence. Taken to the extreme, I can be really stubborn. In some situations, this works for me (my commitment to write this book for you.) In other situations, it works against me (like holding on to a bad feeling.).

Another example is in the famous movie, Star Wars. One of Darth Vader's strengths is his desire for power. Power can be used quite purposefully to serve many people. His need for power was taken to an extreme, however, and his need to have control over others grew. This need eventually became his prison and destroyed him.

"To every disadvantage, there is a corresponding advantage."
W. Clement Stone

When you realize that, yes, you too, are capable of road rage, then you can choose to react differently when the situation comes up and pushes your buttons. When you admit that, yes, you are capable of lying, then you can choose to act differently when a situation occurs in which you might normally lie. There is no bad or good in these scenarios - only choice.

Own the fact that all your feelings are yours and that they are okay. You are fully responsible for everything you feel, whether or not you are consciously aware of your feelings.

Exercise: Your Shadow's Gifts

Your success lies in your ability to ***allow*** yourself to succeed. If, in any way, you believe that success may actually bring you harm, you will not allow yourself to achieve the next level of success. This "defense mechanism" actually is there to protect you.

This exercise is about bringing your strengths to the surface by digging underground first, admitting what you are capable of in the negative sense, and recognizing what you are capable of in the positive sense.

1. Write the 10 worst qualities you can think of about yourself and others, things that you dislike the most. Use descriptive words like explosive, or lazy, or ugly.
2. Make sure you have a complete list before you continue.
3. After each word or phrase, write how each of those qualities actually can be a strength. For example: "I'm impatient." becomes"I get things done, I'm passionate and I care." "I'm lazy." becomes "I'm choosy about where I spend my time and my energy."

____

____

____

____

____

____

____

____

____

____

Examples: If one of your qualities is being "lazy," the strength of being lazy might be considered being choosy about how you spend your time. All the lazy people I know have areas of their lives where they are quite active. Another strength is that a lazy person can be quite stubborn. Plus he or she probably knows how to relax. Being choosy and stubborn can be very positive attributes at the right times and places. "Laziness" is just a word that describes turning up the volume of relaxation, choosiness, and persistence too high, often at the wrong time.

Every attribute has a volume control and each situation requires a different amount of volume. The same attribute in one situation could be beneficial while in another situation it could be harmful. For example, being lazy is useful for a relaxing Sunday afternoon, but not useful at work if you want to keep your job.

If one of your worst qualities is being explosive, you probably are also quite passionate. It is healthy to be passionate if you direct your passion in a positive way. Someone who is sneaky may have the quality of being very observant.

An extreme example is being an addict of any kind. The behavior is destructive, but it does imply certain strengths: being able to escape from pain, and the survival instinct to do whatever it takes to deal with loneliness and the feeling of being out of control.

It is healthy to feel pain. It is also healthy to escape from pain by communing with nature or reading a good book. It is healthy to survive by reaching out for help to recover from addiction. Experiencing pain, escaping pain, and survival are all positive qualities which can be utilized to create a better life.

If you are careless with your diet, you strengths may be the ability to be carefree and spontaneous. It is healthy to be carefree and spontaneous with what you eat... to a degree!

Focusing on the strengths of your shadow does not excuse inappropriate behavior.

Focusing on and acting on the strengths can help you live fully without suppressing natural desires. It is the suppression and lack of acceptance (due to judgment) that leads to madness!

There is a problem with negating the shadow's qualities entirely: you lose the gifts that it has in store for you. Those gifts are necessary for your success. The problem isn't in the qualities of your shadow. The qualities themselves are not bad or good. They are like knives and can be used to cure or to kill. Problems are avoided when you use them wisely and constructively.

The key can be found in three steps: ***awareness, acceptance,*** and ***action***.

Use your shadow's strengths to reach your stars!

Watching You Grow

I feel your pain,
your hurt, your despair,
your sadness,
and I want to kiss you
and hug you and
make it all go away.
But I can't.
And even if I could
I wouldn't really want to.
For in your pain
lies a blessing,
far greater than
the darkness
you feel right now.
My prayer is that
you will open your heart
and allow yourself
to be loved,
so that your past
limitations
can be melted
to reveal
the sacred part of you,
the real you,
that longs to shine
its light on the world.

The Sixth Step

Fertilize the soil.

Chapter 6

Step Forward

Keep going no matter what!

Follow Through

The only way to make a dream come true is to follow through on what you say you'll do. This can be difficult sometimes, especially when there are so many other distractions.

My "Success Team" was powerful (see page 129) because these people expected the best from me, and held me accountable to my dreams. It was hard to show up at each meeting without having made at least some progress. It's such a good feeling when your friends are proud of you! It's an even better feeling knowing you helped someone else achieve what they really wanted.

"We are what we repeatedly do. Excellence, then, is not an act but a habit."
Aristotle

An exercise that truly changed my life and helped me focus on my commitment to live my dreams occurred at a seminar I attended. The presenter asked us to write down one thing – one next step – that we knew we each needed to take in order to make our dreams a reality. I knew I wanted to send a letter to all the authors and mentors in my life, telling them of my commitment to make a positive difference, and thanking them for their inspiration.

After we wrote our next step, we had to make a commitment to the person sitting next to us that we would keep our promise and do what we wrote we would do. The person next to me wasn't sure the step I was taking was small enough; it seemed too challenging to succeed. I made the commitment, though, and kept it. My life has been one big adventure eversince that fateful November day in 1995!

Exercise: Your Next Baby Step

1. Write down one thing you know you need to do to take you to the next step toward the life of your dreams.
2. Make a commitment to do it and give yourself a date it will be accomplished (no later than 72 hours from now).
3. Tell someone else of the promise you have made, and ask them to call you on the date you set to celebrate with you!
4. Give yourself a high five for playing!

Mastering Change - The Power of Play

"Do it wrong." When my friend first heard these words, she did a double-take. She was trying to explain something to me and as I began to write it down, I asked her to repeat herself. She suddenly felt stuck and said she couldn't, that she was going to do it wrong. I said "Do it wrong." When she started to speak again, it came out just right. The pressure to perform was off.

"*Do it wrong!*"
Debbie Cohen

Imagine learning to play the piano. Imagine loving the piano so much that you keep banging on the keys, even though your playing may sound horrible at first. Because you love it, you keep playing more and more often. You're practicing without even trying to. You're learning. Practice becomes play!

When you play this way, you are substituting "play power" for "will power." Will power is no longer needed to create the body shape you desire, the money you want, or the love you intend to experience. Peak performance happens with joy! Act on it! Play!

Try Something New

Somewhere along the way, we learned to focus on our mistakes. For example: minus 10 on your spelling test! What an awful feeling, not exactly inspiring! What about the 10 you got right? We learn to forget to be excited every time we take a step.

Many adults are afraid to try something new because they fear doing it wrong – making a mistake, and looking foolish. This lesson really changed my life. It is the reason I am able to speak in the community to large groups of people over and over again, with the courage to continue, even though I am not perfect.

I've learned that being human is more important than being right, and that it takes ***courage to be imperfect!*** Putting effort into something you enjoy, over and over again, is the key. A child doesn't worry about the mistakes he is making as he learns to walk. He is too busy focusing on the task and enjoying the ride. To make a dream come true will take many steps. If no one else seems to be happy you are taking a step in the right direction, learn to be happy for yourself and join others who have the same innocence.

Embrace Change

Change is happening so rapidly in our society, that it is almost dangerous not to flow with it. Our jobs don't last as long as they used to and our children are growing up faster than they used to. How do we master change? **By embracing it!** The beauty in a waterfall is that it is constantly changing.

Our planet is spinning, whirling around in space. We are living on a moving entity, where change is constant. The weather is changing all the time – more rapidly than ever before. The question is, where can you find security? We have looked to external sources in the past for security – jobs, families, government. No longer do people trust these entities. People aren't sure where to turn.

The best place to turn is within. There's a quiet place in me that knows what is right and good, and consistently guides me in that direction. It keeps me sensitive to what's about to come and, as a result, helps me deal with the changes more effectively.

"That it will never come again is what makes life so sweet."
Emily Dickinson

You've heard of people who can feel in their bodies when a storm is coming? It's the same with change. Stay observant about what is happening around you. What is feeding and nourishing you today may not be there tomorrow, and happily you may find something else more nourishing in the future.

The idea is to know what you want and constantly be on the lookout for better opportunities to bring you closer to your heart's desire. Knowing what you value and what you really want keeps you from attaching yourself to something external, and letting go becomes much easier.

Exercise: Say Cheese!

How do you usually respond to change? In fear, or with ease and joy? One of the best books ever written about mastering change is a parable by Ken Blanchard and Spencer Johnson called, *Who Moved My Cheese?* Read this fun and wisdom-filled story and answer the questions in the back of the book. You will be glad you did!

Life Is a Mystery - Trust It!

Another aspect of mastering change is recognizing that life is a mystery and that everything happens for a reason, even if you don't know what it is. I figure I might as well believe that everything in the world is happening for my highest good and for the highest good of all. It is there as an opportunity to help bring out the best in me. And it is my choice to see it that way. That choice has opened so many doors for me! It makes me seem as though I am lucky, but really it's not luck; it's an attitude of appreciation for everything I have and everything that I don't have.

> ***"There are no mistakes. The events we bring upon ourselves, no matter how unpleasant, are necessary in order to learn what we need to learn; whatever steps we take, they're necessary to reach the places we've chosen to go."***
> Richard Bach

There was a time when I had no idea how I would pay my next month's rent. I was caught up in fear of losing my place to live, my security, everything. One day, desperate for an answer, I borrowed a book on money and prosperity. The writer suggested that I be thankful for not only everything I ***did*** have but for everything that I ***didn't*** have. This was a stretch for me. But I began to realize how to be grateful for my ***experience***. The fact that I don't have something makes my experience uniquely what it is.

As a result, I can relate to those who use money as an excuse not to move forward toward their dreams. I know what it's like, because I've been there. But now, I also know the level of commitment, faith and determination I am capable of.

As a coach, I am much stronger about my convictions. My expectations of people are much higher as well. I look for the best from everyone. I wouldn't be able to be so strong if I hadn't been through the same experience myself to learn the power of perseverance as well as trust the process of life.

Encouragement

Encouragement is one of the most important keys to reaching your stars. "Courage" is the root word. It means seeing fear, and walking forward anyway. It means looking at the bright side of life, and choosing to focus on it. Courage means having the desire to live fully and emotionally to stand on your own two feet. It means knowing you are wonderful, regardless of what happens to you regardless of the mistakes you make.

"What the caterpillar calls a tragedy, the Master calls a butterfly."
Richard Bach

Courage means you are willing to continue to step up to the stage and perform in the main tent of your life, not to spend all your time in side shows and distractions. It means doing what you were born to do and reaching out to help others, knowing you DO make a difference.

Encouragement also means not doing anything for someone else that he or she can do for themselves. It means standing back and allowing your child to fall down, to fail, to make mistakes and to feel the pain, so that she can feel okay about herself. She now knows that as she gets older and makes new mistakes, she will have the confidence to bounce back quickly. It means not hovering, but letting go and trusting.

The Legend of The Thousand Demons

I once heard a story told of the "Ceremony of the Thousand Demons." It is a legend told of Hindu monks who participate in a ceremony held only once every hundred years. By successfully completing this ceremony, each monk would achieve eternal enlightenment. However, if he was unsuccessful, he would die.

The ceremony required each monk walk through the "room of the thousand demons." This was a magical room. After the door was closed and locked behind the monk, he would experience his worst fears in 3-dimensional form. If he was afraid of heights, he'd find himself standing on a cliff. Fear of snakes? They'd be crawling all around and on him. Mice? Poverty? Illness? Rejection? Whatever the monk held in his mind as a fear, would manifest itself and appear to him as real.

Each monk practiced a lifetime to go through this ceremony, and he would have only one chance. There were few who succeeded.

Those who did achieve eternal enlightenment were asked to reveal the secret to their success. They shared these two:

"Effort only fully releases its reward after a person refuses to quit."
Napoleon Hill

First, no matter what fear came up, the monk would acknowledge it and then confidently say, "That's not real. That's not real. That's not real."

The monk acknowledged the fear *before* stating that it wasn't real. He did not deny its existence, only its reality in his life.

Second, he ***kept his feet moving forward,*** no matter what!

Exercise: Face Your Demons

Write three fears you allowed to keep you from moving forward and achieving what you really want.

Write yourself a letter or a note, stating your commitment to move forward, toward your dreams – no matter what!

Create a specific action plan to overcome one of your fears and do it!

Do Something Different!

I'm choosy about the type of people I spend time with. Everyone I come into contact with influences me, and I influence them. I try to surround myself with people who have good intentions, are positive and behave in ways to show they care.

This does not mean that relationships are always rosy. It is easier, though, when we're committed to working together to find win-win solutions. Sometimes this can be difficult and requires a lot of good communication, but when people are committed to living this way, we do whatever we can to work things out. Read Stephen R. Covey's book, The 7 Habits of Highly Effective People, to learn more about creating win-win agreements.

Pain and growth are part of life. No one is perfect. Relationships get sticky at times, and you may not always be sure how to respond to the person or situation. Try this: When you don't know what to do, DO SOMETHING DIFFERENT!

So often in relationships, we're caught in cycles of behaviors that feel crazy. When people complain about something in their relationship, it is usually about something that has been happening over and over and over, maybe even for years. You don't have to analyze too much to make a change to transform the entire scene. Simply DO **ONE THING** DIFFERENT, and the ***entire*** cycle will change.

"Associate yourself with men of quality if you esteem your own reputation, for 'tis better to be alone than in bad company."

George Washington

The enticing thing about this is, if it doesn't work, you can always try something else. REACH OUT and ask other people for help! Be patient with yourself. It took Thomas Edison nearly 10,000 trials to create the light bulb! And how long have you been a child, a parent, or a leader? Continue trying new things as you move forward.

I once read a funny story about a married woman in her 80's who dealt creatively with her husband's annoying behavior. Every evening, she would cook and serve dinner to her husband, who would come to the table without a shirt. This habit bothered her because she didn't want to look at his chest while she ate. She thought it was quite rude, and she asked him repeatedly to wear a shirt to dinner. He continued his behavior, and she became more irritated. She decided to DO SOMETHING DIFFERENT. She cooked dinner and, before serving it, she bared her chest and sat down to eat with her husband. He quickly got the message and put on a shirt, and he has worn one to dinner ever since.

Exercise: Do Something Different!

Identify a specific problem that you're having in communicating or relating with another person. How does the scenario begin? For this to work, you must identify **BEHAVIORS** and **FEELINGS**, ***not* ATTITUDES** or your interpretations of what is happening will be confusing. For example:

- Behaviors: he *slammed* the door, she *yelled*
- Feelings: I felt *angry or frustrated or hurt*
- Attitudes: she was *rude*, he was *obnoxious*

"Grant me the serenity to accept the things I cannot change, The courage to change the things I can, and the wisdom to know the difference."
Reinhold Neibuhr

1. In the problem you've identified, what usually happens first? Second? Third? Etc. (Number them). Continue writing until your list represents the situation in its completion.

2. Circle the numbers from the list where you are able to make a change. Remember, you cannot control another person. You can only decide for yourself what you will change, so look closely. Draw an arrow circling from the bottom number to the top one, representing the cycle or pattern.

3. Identify what you could do differently in those areas you circled.

4. Practice letting go of any resentment, blame or attempts to change what is not in your control (other people's behavior).

5. If you truly see that ***you also participate*** in the unfolding of situations, then you ***can*** shape the outcomes that you want.

If you have made a concerted effort to get a better result in a relationship, and that result does not happen, ask yourself how important it is to you. It may be necessary to let go of your expectations of the outcome or remove yourself from the relationship. Read the section in Chapter 7 titled "Release Attachment."

The Seventh Step

Continue to nurture and feed your dream.

Prune the branches to keep it strong and healthy.

Chapter 7

Reach Out! Team Up!

Ask for what you want and reach out to help others.

Chapter 7

My First Success Team & How It Worked

I first learned about coaching in a seminar for building personal power. Everyone who has a dream needs a coach – someone to encourage and hold you accountable, offering suggestions and feedback along the way. *Every* professional athlete, in every sport, including the Olympic games, has a coach. **NO ONE** gets to the top alone. NO ONE!

My dream was to write a book and so I wanted to find my coach. Before the internet, finding the right one was extremely time consuming. So I called together a group of friends who were working on their own goals and dreams and created a "success team" instead. One of the team members' goal was to move to a new home, another - to get married. The third member wanted to travel more, and I wanted to write a book. We met with the intent of helping each other reach our goals through encouragement, accountability and suggestions. We became each other's coach.

At our first meeting, we each told of our dreams. Later, we created collages – "treasure maps" of our dreams by cutting out magazine pictures, allowing our imaginations to run wild.

We met every two weeks. Each member had 20 minutes to discuss two things:

1. During the last two weeks did you accomplish what your were committed to do.

2. What baby steps are you going to take now?

If a step was too big, we could suggest making it smaller. If someone wasn't sure what to do next, we'd help by offering options.

What made the group work was our commitment to show up, and stay on track with our questions during these sessions. The experience was incredible as we moved past our own comfort zones and closer to the lives of our dreams. We became success teammates!

"Everyone needs to be valued. Everyone has the potential to give something back."
Diana - Princess of Wales

It was fun looking out for each other, holding each other's dreams in our hearts and thoughts while going about our personal lives. It was exciting to watch people break out of their cocoons to fly!

The world is filled with people to reach out to. You will reach your stars more quickly and easily by uniting forces with positive and like-minded people.

Chapter 7

Coaches & Mentors

A mentor is someone you can trust to encourage and guide you to develop who you are. Mentors are those you can have a personal relationship with - someone who can hold your hand as you journey through life.

A coach can be a mentor, even someone you've never met. For example, a friend of mine, who is a great polo player, says she learned how to play by watching polo players on television. Those players "coached" her by modeling correct behavior and tactics. And yet, she's never met those players. Many authors, seminar leaders, and television personalities like Oprah Winfrey have coached me by "showing" me a other ways.

My Aunt Ruth was a great mentor to me because she *listened* to me; she did not always agree with me, but she never criticized me. She made me feel important by showing me how to relate to others with patience and understanding. She accepted me for who I am.

Who has been a coach or mentor to you – a family member, a teacher, a trusted friend? What qualities did she or he have that influenced your life for the better?

"Everybody can be great . . .
because anybody can serve.
You don't have to have
a college degree to serve.
You don't have to make your
subject and verb agree to serve.
You only need to have a heart
full of grace and a
soul generated by love."

Martin Luther King, Jr.

Exercise: Connect with a Coach or Mentor

Think about someone who has been a coach or mentor to you. What made that person great in your eyes? Did you ever try to be like him or her? How did he or she make you feel? What gifts did you receive? Write to that person and thank them for making a positive difference in your life.

Most likely, this person gave you a sense of hope and a feeling that you are okay the way you are. Maybe he or she saw something better in you than you could see in yourself. This is the primary aim of any coach or mentor; for only with that vision can they be of any use in guiding someone to better their life or their skill. They must be able to experience that person achieving it and believe that it is possible.

As a coach myself, sometimes this is difficult, especially when the person doesn't look the part they are asking me to help them reach. When that happens to me, I ask myself, "Who are you to judge what another person is capable of being? Look how far you've come in your own life. No one would ever have guessed all that you have accomplished." This gives me the motivation to seek the best in others, regardless of the distractions and facades that may cover up their best selves.

Being a mentor inspires me to continually seek the best in myself, and to take consistent steps toward living my best self. People learn best by example, which inspires me to constantly motivate myself to reach the next step. The more steps I climb by reaching my dreams, the more people I can touch. Everyone benefits.

Create Awesome Relationships

In 10th grade I made a life-changing decision. In my family, hugs and compliments were rare. This was not due to a lack of love, but rather to what my parents and their parents had been taught. This was very hard for me, because I wanted love to be more openly expressed. And yet, there was so much fear of getting hurt that often I held back, just as I was taught. Then I would rebel and act out in unhealthy ways in order to get attention.

"*Too often we underestimate the power of a touch, a smile, a kind word, a listening ear, an honest compliment, or the smallest act of caring, all of which have the potential to turn a life around.*"
Leo Buscaglia

In order to live a happier, more openly loving lifestyle, I decided to change. I purchased a book called How to Start A Conversation and Make Friends by Don Gavor. After reading some of the ideas in the book, I made a commitment to go to school the next day, take a step out of my shell, and give somebody a compliment. I had no idea to whom, or how the words would come out of my mouth, but I was determined.

The opportunity appeared during 2nd period English class. I was sitting at my desk when Marie walked in the room. She was wearing a gorgeous blue satin dress, and she looked absolutely phenomenal! I remember holding the words in my throat, before telling her, "Marie, you look really pretty in that dress." Those words were so difficult for me, I could hardly stand it. And yet, I had conquered my fear! She thanked me, and the moment passed.

My friend Mike says that he believes we all have a secret: *We all know we want love and we want to give love. But we keep this a secret from each other. We pretend that it doesn't matter. But down deep we know that it does.*

Who do you know that could benefit from an uplifting compliment, a hug or a smile? It's positively contagious!

Build a Strong Community

Schools, businesses, organizations and individuals make up a community. In a healthy, strong community, the links between people are strong.

Exploration, discovery, reflection and joy are keys to a complete education at any age. Exploration leads to discovery. Exploring and discovering one's outer world and reflecting upon the experience in one's inner world, are the foundation for learning.

"*Children are the most important asset in a country.*"
Nelson Mandela

People cannot explore in a vacuum. Everyone is born with a unique talent and gift, something they can do better than anyone else in the world. Exploring is the only way to discover what it could be. Exploring enables us to reach out and create a strong community. Individuals, schools ,businesses and organizations make up the whole.

Schools cannot succeed alone. It takes a community to raise a child. Our community will prosper as students are better prepared for the real world. By interacting in the business world now, they will have more reasons to study!

Businesses cannot succeed alone, it takes a community to build a business. Schools are a phenomenal network of people and can support businesses that care about kids.

Everyone can reach out to local schools and mentor the students. Speak to the kids about what you do and what your day is like. Inspire them. Tell them the challenges you face and how you found solutions. Teach the importance of passion behind intelligence. Invite a student to work with you for a day. Adopt a classroom. Be there. Attend school programs. Mentor the teachers and students by sharing your skills for a project that they are doing (for example, a printing company can help students with graphic design). Students and teachers love it when you simply participate with them. Be patient.

Interviewing teenagers, I found that many of the teen leaders want their peers to learn tolerance; to be kind and sensitive to other people's differences. They realize that bullying and putting other people down is detrimental to feeling safe and to learning. Tolerance can be taught when students can understand another person's experience. Bring in speakers who have overcome issues like drug addiction and disabilities. Have them share with the students what it is like to be in their shoes and deal with the challenges they face. Have the children write essays and poems describing their reactions and feelings, allowing all emotions to be expressed with no judgment. It is important for the students to know they are supported for being themselves and to not be ashamed of their emotions. The goal is acceptance – of one's own feelings first and then others'.

The children will be inspired to reach out and make a difference. Encourage their efforts by saying YES and showing them the way. Allow them to teach you the beauty of youthful dreams while you help them make it happen. They need your help with the logistics! Let them know they make a difference.

Schools can celebrate and thank their community partners with awards, ribbons, letters from the children, and phone calls of thanks. Appreciation makes a difference and encourages people to continue giving.

Parents and community members, support your teachers! Donate materials that can be used in the classroom. Find out what a classroom needs and be creative with what you give. A publicly held company can bring the teachers an annual report for the students to analyze. A field trip to your place of business and a discount for teachers are great ideas. Our teachers are today's heroes and they deserve lots of appreciation!

Here's one suggestion for reaching out not only to the community but to the world – it's in international organization called "The Earth Charter." The Earth Charter is a "declaration of fundamental principles for building a just, sustainable, and peaceful global society in the 21st Century." It seeks to inspire in all peoples a new sense of global interdependence and shared responsibility for the well-being of the human family and the larger living world. It is an expression of hope and a call to create a global partnership at a critical juncture in history."

The Earth Charter Community Summits are annual gatherings to inspire ordinary people to make the principles of the Earth Charter a reality in their lives and in their communities. For more information or to get involved in the Earth Charter Community Summits, please visit their website at ***www.earthcharter.org*** or ***www.earthchartersummits.org***.

Chapter 7

The Greatest Gift

People want to feel important, and the greatest gift you can give another person is to let them know just how important and appreciated they are. One of the best ways to show it is by being "fully present" with that person.

When it is sincere, this gift is one of the most appreciated gifts in the world. It may seem to be a very uncomfortable gift to give – only because we are not used to interacting so openly, closely, and sincerely with others.

Closeness and appreciation are natural needs. We see these needs reflected in the desires of infants and small children when we share tenderness with them. As adults, we have the same needs.

Most people enjoy being appreciated - even when expressed openly. Though some may push away at first because it feels uncomfortable. People I've worked with first acted "professional" by pushing away my affection and appreciation. Now they greet *me* with a warm hug. I have seen this transformation over and over again, in friends, family, colleagues, and clients.

"You can't cure every patient, but you can care for every patient."
Patch Adams

The beauty is that we all have this capacity to connect more deeply with others by expanding our comfort zone.

The love you give is your greatest gift.

Voice Mail

One of my favorite new technologies is the voice mail system. I seem to have created a signature with my friends by leaving them voice mail messages telling them how wonderful they are, and how much I believe in them and in their dreams.

More than a few times, I have heard the comment from people with answering machines, "I wish I had voice mail, so that I could have saved the message you sent me. It made me feel so good. I kept it as long as I could but I had to finally erase it!" Or from people with voice mail, "I am still listening to that message you left me. Thank you so much. I really needed to hear that."

Send someone an encouraging voice mail today!

"If you want your children to improve, let them overhear the nice things you say about them to others."

Haim Ginott

What Do You Expect?

It's funny how people will live up to your expectations of them. One thing that drives me crazy is when parents tell me what horrible children they have – while their children are standing right there. Well, of course the kids would act out. This is true for children as well as for many adults.

Remember – what you focus your attention on grows stronger. People often act exactly the way you expect them to act. This is called "self-fulfilling prophecy."

Many studies have been done of teachers and their expectations of their students. Amazingly, and consistently, the children lived up to what their teacher believed about them, and this was reflected in their grades as well as their behaviors!

What do you expect of your students or your employees? What do you expect of your bosses or your teachers? What do you expect of yourself?

"However much we guard against it, we tend to shape ourselves in the image others have of us."

Eric Hoffer

Chapter 7

Release Attachments

Attachment comes from fear that you will lose something or that you won't get something. Be careful not to allow yourself to become attached to your expectations. This will take you out of the present moment, wasting precious time and energy. By focusing too heavily on the future, you will not be able to perform at your peak while in the present.

There are so many variables that can effect how things turn out. Attachment to a particular result, in any situation, can lead to feelings of disappointment if your wished-for result doesn't happen. It can lead to a feeling to control or be in charge of other people's actions. But, when you do what seems to be the appropriate footwork in any given situation, and don't hold on to a particular outcome, you know you did your best. Hold your vision high, make a decision, do the next right step, then let go.

Most people have their strongest attachment to relationships. As you grow, some of your friends will support you while others resist your changes. This is normal. Know what you value. A strong "yes" to a path you value will make it easier to say "no" to lesser paths.

"I can honestly say that I was never affected by the question of the success of an undertaking. If I felt it was the right thing to do, I was for it regardless of possible outcome."
Golda Meir

For example, letting go of destructive relationships may be necessary to reaching your stars. This is one of the toughest challenges people face. When I used to counsel addicts, it was amazing how difficult it was for the clients to release unhealthy friendships and relationships in their neighborhoods. This was home for them and letting go of drugs meant also letting go of what felt safe and familiar to them.

There are people who do not want to or are not ready to take responsibility for their lives and happiness. In those cases, you must decide if it is best to continue to participate in the relationship or if it's time to move forward without them.

Let go of your attachments and you will be better able to accept what is, to make better decisions, live more peacefully with the results, and learn from your experiences.

Exercise: Release Attachments

Think about how you're holding your dreams inside of you. Are you holding them so tightly that if they don't turn out just the way you expect them to, you'll be devastated? Or are you holding your dreams loosely enough to be open to life's gifts?

My cousin Michelle, a diabetic since the age of three, decided to get pregnant at the age of 29. She was a very high risk case. She held a positive attitude throughout the pregnancy while being realistically unsure how far she'd be able to make it. In fact, her mother and sister would buy clothing and diapers for the baby-to-be, and Michelle would say with a smile "Thanks! And make sure to keep the receipts." She was brave to acknowledge her fears and move forward positively anyway. It is a joy to report that she did give birth to a healthy baby girl!

Detachment can allow you to see the blessing in disguise because it gives you an open mind. When rock climbing, one must grab onto the next stone while letting go of the last one in order to move forward safely. Letting go is as important as grabbing on.

In which areas of your life are you experiencing detachment? In which areas of your life are you experiencing attachment? What steps can you take to let go of attachment and free yourself?

You know you're attached if you find yourself obsessing or stressing over a particular result. If this is the case for you, STOP!, let go, and focus your attention on something you do have control over (like doing the dishes). Ask yourself "What's the next right step?" and do it!

Communicate Often and Openly

Have you ever taken a blind trust walk, where one person is blindfolded and the other is sighted, and the sighted person guides the blindfolded person? It's a game of trust. For the blindfolded person to feel safe in that game requires good communication.

Communication is not just verbal; in fact you are always communicating. One study by Mehrabian & Ferris (1967) suggested that what people "hear" most when you are speaking is your non-verbal behaviors. They found when people are receiving information from another person, they retain only 7% of what is actually being said (verbal), 38% of how it is said (vocal), and 55% of what the body language reflects (facial expression). People receive more information from your body language and tone of voice than what you actually say!

In order to get through the blind trust walk without any verbal communication allowed (except for laughing!), the participants must touch each other to guide the "blind" person. Trust is built when communication is consistent and perceived as helpful and kind. Most people like to know the people surrounding them are trustworthy and care about their well-being. Trust also requires accountability and people keeping their word.

When a feeling of trust is created, it is much easier to focus on the task at hand (work, school, enjoying each other). Achieving this feeling directly relates to the ability of a person or organization to reach greater successes.

"...Love is the opening door, love is what we came here for..."

Elton John

Chapter 7

Speak Your Truth

Trust is the foundation of a healthy relationship, and open communication is the key ingredient. In relationships, much of the time, we have no idea and often assume what another person is thinking or feeling. Why not just ask and communicate?

Wondering what another person is thinking creates worry. When assuming what another person is thinking, most people assume the negative. If you believe someone has a negative thought about you, you may feel more closed off to them – even if your assumption isn't true.

Worrying is the opposite of innocence, openness, and trust. Speaking your mind, even if the other person might not understand or like it – it is the best way to honor your feelings. Honoring your feelings is a function of loving yourself!

THIS IS IMPORTANT: Speaking your mind is not an excuse to dump your hurt or anger on another person. If your intention is to solve a situation or to heal it, and you do your best to express yourself with that intention in mind, that is wonderful. But many people take "expressing yourself" to mean that they can just vent their anger at anyone they choose, however they choose and whenever they choose.

This is not healthy communication. It belittles and breaks the human spirit. We can all speak from experience. We've all spoken out in anger at our children, our pets, and ourselves. Words are sometimes remembered years after they are spoken and can leave a strong imprint.

Speaking your mind clearly and openly takes practice. Communicate with the intent of creating a win-win situation. Do not be discouraged if you don't get it right the first time. Keep at it, and remember to focus your intent on love which is ultimately what you want in return.

"I can trust my friends. These people force me to examine, encourage me to grow."

Cher

Exercise: Relationship Nourishment

A relationship is like a flower. It needs sunshine, water, and healthy soil for it to grow. The following exercise can help you nourish the relationships in your life.

Think of a relationship in your life that is working well or has worked well. Focus on the strengths you have already developed. What is the sunshine and water that you are providing? Is it phone calls or letters or prayers? Do you smile around that person? Do you listen? How do you positively acknowledge that person?

Think of a relationship in your life that is not working well, one that you want to improve. What sunshine and nourishment are you using to improve the signals you are sending? You can't control the other person, but you can decide what you are willing to give or not to give. How do you want to see yourself behave? What would make you feel most loving?

Sometimes we get stuck in relationships where we are not sure how to make it better. We must ask ourselves: have I gone through all the options and ways to improve it? Is the ball now in the other person's court? When you feel really unsure, you can send that person love through your thoughts, and pray for peace.

Reflection: *Ask yourself: Do I choose peace or conflict? Do I want to be happy or do I want to be right? Which will lead to greater closeness? So much of the difficulty in our relationships comes from the need to be right. If you let go of that need, how much would the quality of your relationships improve? How much more inner peace would you have? What is your intent?*

Chapter 7

The Boy Who Lived in a Shoe

There once was a boy who lived in a shoe
He was bored and didn't know what to do.
He wanted a boat and a truck and a house
But all he had was a little pet mouse.
He'd eat whatever he could find
He spoke to no one and kept his own mind.
Then one day he fell down into the gutter
And a family helped him up and gave him fresh water.
He did not know what to think of this act
For he never spoke to anyone and that was a fact.
But they seemed nice and very sweet
So he told them all his dreams and they gave him a treat.
It wasn't a candy bar or a toy
But it was a secret for the lonely boy.
You can't stay alone forever, young lad;
They were right and he knew it and he was glad.
So he had a party with his newfound friends
And together they figured out how to make the best blends.
For he had great taste buds and it was true
Chocolate and strawberries make a great stew!
So they took their concoction to the local store
And the smiling manager greeted them at the door.
We have a very yummy drink
You'll see it now, it's brown and pink.
And the tall, grinning man so loved the taste
That he gulped it all down and none went to waste.
He asked them if he could buy 100 cases
And they made it and their smiles glowed on their faces.
And the little boy, you know,
The one who wanted a boat and a truck and a house?
He got all that and brought along his mouse.
But the best part for him was his newfound friends
Who stayed with him and played with him until the end.

The Eighth Step

Enjoy the fruits!

Chapter 8

Celebrate!

Reflect on your accomplishments.

Dreams come true!

Celebration

Celebrate for getting to the end of this book! Celebrate for being a unique human being! Celebrate for choosing to wake up this morning! Celebrate for choosing to nap! Celebrate being alive! YOU ARE AWESOME! You were born that way! How could you not be?

Adults in our culture often feel the need to have a reason to celebrate a graduation, wedding, birthday, etc. . . or think they should wait for the end result to happen first. There is so much formality, and oftentimes, pressure surrounding a celebration.

"A light heart lives long."
William Shakespeare

Young children, on the other hand, celebrate often and easily. They clap their hands, sing, dance, yell! They celebrate the smallest things. Watch them at a circus or in the park. Their enthusiasm is contagious. They are innocent and natural in their celebrations.

We have so much to learn from them by noticing the joyful things in life and appreciating them. For example, lighting a candle, feeling the softness of a comforter, watching the branches in the trees sway in the wind, noticing our child do something new. Celebration is that FEELING that spontaneously occurs when we place our attention on these wondrous experiences.

That feeling also happens when we've done something well. It is interesting to watch a team who has done a job and is truly satisfied with it. There's almost a glow in the air. It's not something that can be placed there, it just happens. People's eyes are lit and there is a feeling of excitement.

The process of reaching your stars allows for so much celebration because you are doing what you enjoy! Celebration allows us to reinforce what we have done well! Let's celebrate what's right and watch it grow!

Exercise: How Do You Celebrate? - Your Personal View

Write your answers to the following questions: What does celebrate mean to you? What makes something a celebration? Think back to celebrations you really enjoyed. What made them celebrations?

Webster's Definition of "Celebrate"

Webster's New Universal Unabridged Dictionary (1996) defines ***celebrate:*** 1. to observe (a day or commemorate (an event) with ceremonies or festivities 2. to make known publicly; proclaim 3. to praise widely or to present to widespread and favorable public notice, as through newspapers c novels 4. to perform with appropriate rites and ceremonies; solemnize 5. to perform a religious ce emony 6. to have or participate in a party.

What surprised me the most were definitions "2" and "3": to make known publicly; proclaim; to praise widely or to present widespread and favorable public notice.

When was the last time you proclaimed what is so wonderful about yourself? When was the last time you asked someone else about his improvements, efforts, or positive changes?

"Follow your bliss."
Joseph Campbell

Most of us associate such proclamation with arrogance or bragging. It is quite uncomfortable for many people. I think we need a lot more of it! Let's share good news on a regular basis and celebrate those who share it. Children know how to do this. They are innocent when they exclaim, "Look at me! See what I can do!" Famous musicians, artists and athletes do this. The proclamation does not necessarily have to be loud; it can be subtle, such as giving someone a homemade gift or inviting them to enjoy your cooking.

Observe others: How many people do you know who enjoy sharing good news? How do you feel when they do?

Observe yourself: How comfortable do you feel sharing really great news with another persor Do you enjoy telling others about a positive change you made or a skill that you are in the proces of developing, or of the insights and growth you have recently experienced?

Celebrate Our Schools!

The best marketers in the world and the people who sell the most goods are great at proclaiming the strengths of their product publicly and loudly for everyone to hear. They are great at tooting their own horns!

I have a dream where the media focuses on what our schools do well and creates massive positive publicity by sharing all their accomplishments with the public!

"Sometimes our light goes out, but is blown into flame by another human being. Each of us owes great thanks to those who have rekindled this light.
Albert Schweitzer

Every school should have a public relations specialist and expert marketer to inform the community of all of the wonderful things that are happening there: the improvements students are making, new classes the teachers are creating, upcoming events, and really get specific and shout about ***what's going* RIGHT!**

Our principals, teachers and students are the silent heroes of our world. They are developing our future and it is up to each one of us to honor, acknowledge and celebrate them! I wonder what it would do to our children's level of motivation if a child or teacher was acknowledged publicly every day for making the world a better place. I wonder what would happen if we celebrated our children and educators as boldly and beautifully as we celebrate our sports teams. *What we focus our attention on will* **GROW!**

Focus on What Is Right

It is time to focus on the positive steps and accomplishments that people are making rather than putting on extreme pressure to make the grade.

The desire to participate is a positive natural tendency. It is why young children volunteer to sing or dance without hesitation. They haven't learned of the need to pressure themselves to do it right. They celebrate each step fully! They know they can! When people are happy, they make the grade or increase the profit because they want to!

Permission Letter

In order to live in the present, inspiring spontaneous action, I've found that giving myself permission to live outside the box is very helpful. And so I give this gift to you!

"You only live once – but if you work it right once is enough."
Joe E. Lewis

Dear Friend,

You have permission to celebrate like a child.

You have permission to proclaim, in writing or verbally, good things happening in your life.

You have permission to focus your energy on what's right and wonderful and good, with the innocence of childhood.

You have permission to laugh too loud.

You have permission to have as much fun playing as you want; to squeeze every moment from this life.

You have permission to bang on the piano, even when it sounds horrible. As much as others complain, they know that they are too embarrassed to do the same and will try to stop you. Keep playing! Encourage them to try something new, to remember the experience of what it's like to learn – the joy as well as the frustration.

You have permission to explore new things.

You have permission to be surprised at what you discover.

You have permission to get into trouble now and then.

You have permission to purchase the Kool & the Gang CD *and dance to* "Celebration!"

You have permission to make a silly face in the mirror until you actually laugh!

You have permission to give 100% of yourself in whatever you choose to do.

Your good friend,

Debbie

Exercise: "Dear Me"

Write yourself a letter of permission to celebrate! You can use the previous one as a guide.

Carpé Diem! - Seize the Day

<u>DO IT NOW!</u> Reaching your stars takes time! If you wait for things to be completely done, you'll ***<u>never</u>*** celebrate. There is always something left to do. The big projects take so long to finish. The little projects seem to be endless, and before you finish one, you're beginning another.

So, you can celebrate all the time! Hi-five yourself! Sing! Do a happy dance! Take time to reflect on what you ***<u>have</u>*** done so far! Say YES!!!

"As long as I continue to hear from 'normal' people telling me I am too childish, I know I'm doing just fine."
Dr. Wayne Dyer

I find myself celebrating in all kinds of places, at any given moment. For example, when I walk into a large discount shopping store, I might bounce the balls or check out the latest gadgets or dance to the music. I can't help but have a little bit of a joy in my step as I walk through the colorful aisles of ideas and choices someone created for me! One of my favorite aisles is the office products – pens and markers of all shapes and colors delight me to no end. It is like a creative feast! No matter which way I turn, I seem to find something to be excited about.

Life is like a big store. The world offers so many possibilities and we get to choose the things we enjoy the most. There is virtually no end to the things we could be celebrating.

<u>The benefits of celebrating:</u>

- ★ Celebration feels great!
- ★ It's relaxing.
- ★ It keeps things in perspective. Most worries are not life or death.
- ★ You can feel full and complete no matter what your life situation seems to be.
- ★ You create great memories and many happy moments.
- ★ You remember that you are wonderful.
- ★ Your feelings of joy and gratitude increase.
- ★ It's contagious!

<u>The fear:</u> You might feel foolish.

<u>The solution: So what? Go for it!</u>

Chapter 8

Aborigine Birthdays & My Birthday Party

I enjoy the description in the book Mutant Message Down Under, by Marlo Morgan where the aborigines have a personalized custom for celebration. They do not celebrate birthdays or holidays. They think this is silly because you really have no control over those things. Those dates are just that – dates; they are not events.

On the other hand, when one of them feels that he or she has made significant progress or has experienced growth in a particular area of his or her life, a public announcement is made by that person, and they celebrate together in song and dance.

Young children do this naturally! So can we.

A party creates a space and time to be with our friends.

One of my happiest celebrations was my 30th birthday, a surprise party at a children's indoor and outdoor game room and fun center. My first surprise was watching my adult friends, one by one, walk through the door carrying birthday presents for me (no children in this group). Once we were all seated, I opened my presents, to find that they were all TOYS!

During our bubble gum-blowing contest,the family at the table next to us were trying to guess whose birthday it was. They were totally perplexed and kept waiting for kids to come join us. Eventually they figured out that it was my birthday. Later that evening, one of the mothers said that she loved the idea and that she was going to have her birthday party there next year!

"Life is better when it's fun. Boy, that's deep, isn't it?"
Kevin Costner

Her little boy was staring at us with such curiosity. He came over and asked me if he could open one of my presents. I remember him grinning from ear-to-ear when I said yes. After he opened the gift, he asked me if he could keep it. I said okay, and thought he would burst with joy!

It was a fantastic celebration of unfettered fun and silly presents that made me smile all evening. It is one celebration that I will remember forever because we felt that childlike carefree innocence again.

Gratitude

I am grateful for all that I have and all that I don't have. I am grateful for all that I am and all that I am becoming. Life is good.

I have learned to be constantly grateful. This means celebrating what I do have and who I am ***right now***. This lesson, more than any other, has helped me get out of personal ruts and into creating wonderful experiences.

One of my favorite exercises to keep myself feeling upbeat and energized is a "Gratitude Journal." Writing makes me think about and affirm, every day, all that I have and all that I am choosing to perceive as wonderful and good. I have also used this journal to affirm that I ***do*** make a difference, by writing down the positive things I do that touch other's lives. This is a WOW! of an experience for me.

Exercise: Your Gratitude Journal

Write five "WOWs!" and five "THANKS!" every day.

Make this a bedtime habit. You'll feel much more peaceful as you fall asleep. Your perceived value of who you are will also increase, as will your contributions. You will find that more good things begin to happen for you.

1. Write five things you did that made a difference in someone else's life. Did you make someone smile? Did you give someone your ears? Did you give an extra tip to the waitress? Did you maintain a positive attitude in a stressful situation?

2. Write five things for which you are thankful. Examples: Your shoelaces, your ability to breathe, your ability to read, your child, the money that you have, or even the money that you don't have. (Yes, you can celebrate that, too, for the lessons that you are learning!) Stretch your mind. This exercise will change your life forever!

"Everyone has inside him a piece of good news. The good news is that you don[illegible] know how great you can be! How much you can love! Wha[illegible] you can accomplish! And wha[illegible] your potential is!"

Anne Frank

Good night and sweet dreams!

"The secret to happiness is to count your blessings."

William Penn

Total Success Daily Affirmations

1. CLEAR MIND - *Inner Silence and "Peek State"*

I choose a positive attitude. I clear my mind daily and when making important decisions. The choices I make today become my reality tomorrow. My heart is full. My intentions are clear. I ask fo guidance and honor the guidance that I receive. I trust that the universe has only good and compassionate intentions for me.

2. TIME - *My Values and Priorities*

I am consciously on a journey of self-discovery. I know my likes, dislikes, values and passions and I prioritize my time wisely as a result. I am in touch with and responsive to the desires of my soul. I have a gift: there is something I can do better than anyone else in the whole world, and my most important job is to discover what it is and share it. I experience true freedom; I have integrit with myself and enthusiasm for life!

3. HEALTH - *My Body and Spirit*

I cleanse and release my emotions regularly. My nutritional program is cleansing. When making life decisions, I take my age into consideration so that my more "youthful" dreams are acted upon in time, if possible. I feel vibrant, energized, flexible and strong. I have a good sense of humor!

4. RELATIONSHIP *with* PEOPLE - *Including Self*

The present is a gift and I appreciate each moment. I am grateful for all of the people in my life. The more love I give and receive, the more full I feel. I assume the best in myself and others and act "as if." I thoughtfully and kindly express my words, feelings and actions. I forgive easily an grow with every experience. I feel a sense of belonging, connected, compassion and love.

5. RELATIONSHIP *with* ENVIRONMENT

My environment inspires me to positive, focused action. My home and my work area are well organized and uncluttered. This allows me to have a clear mind. I take care of my belongings in good time (cars, dishes, finances...), and prevent urgencies as much as possible. I am self-reliant. I have more time to live in the creative zone, rather than the reactive zone. I feel satisfied.

6. WORK - *Vocation, Career, Hobby*

I joyfully serve and contribute to the betterment of humanity. I do what I love and I love what I do. I follow my bliss and my needs are always taken care of. I am open to new ideas. I am supported for living my passion and giving fully. I care.

7. MONEY - *Worldly Success*

I earn, save, and invest money wisely. Money is energy. I spend, tithe, and invest money with joy. My debts are paid easily. I trust the flow of money, and I am open and receptive to all good. My relationship with money is based on the desires of my soul. I am fully supported for doing what I love, I am free.

Total Success Habits Checklist

'eek Date:__________________ Week Number_________

"Total success" is having the ability and the confidence to be who you really are.
Photocopy this checklist and write in it daily. Review it on the same day every week for 12 weeks.
Check each blank as you complete it. Please read chapters 1, 2 & 3 first.

TEP 1. BREATHE

___ Take deep breaths today through relaxation or through exercise.

TEP 2. EXPLORE

___ Learn something new today.
___ Write in your journal to explore and discover your inner self.
___ Write ONE question that you are currently pondering; a life mystery:

____

TEP 3. DECIDE

___ Decide your attitude for the day. Feel it moving through your body.

TEP 4. BUILD CONFIDENCE

___ Daydream and imagine yourself doing something well today. Feel it.

TEP 5. BALANCE

___ Feel, accept and release some of your emotions today. Feel positive emotions replacing them.

TEP 6. STEP FORWARD

___ Take one small step toward one of your big dreams. Feel it happening.

TEP 7. REACH OUT

___ Give encouragement, or ask for it.

TEP 8. CELEBRATE!

___ Feel AWESOME! Write 5 examples of what you are thankful for:

ore suggestions:

___ Each week, review your past week and set the stage for next week. What step did you do well last week? What strength, personality trait, or habit do you want to improve next week?
___ Start a success group and meet weekly to share your progress with like-minded people. Celebrate your success!
___ Spend an hour by yourself each week, doing something fun and different for you.

★ ★ ★ ★ ★ ★ ★ ★

Special Thanks to

Sue Bley / Bley Advertising & Design
405 Central Ave. Suite 208, St. Petersburg, FL 33701 / (727) 866-0068 / sbley@interaccess.net

Willy Mathes / Writing Coach & Editor
418 W. Louisiana Avenue, Tampa, FL 33603 / (813) 232-2946 / wmathes@tampabay.rr.com

Jim Walters / Kichita Productions: Publishing Services for Creative Authors
227 Shadehill Court, Tampa, FL 33612 / (813) 931-5148 / kichita001@excite.com

Sylvia Hemmerly / Publishing Professional
10002 Hilltop Drive, New Port Richey, FL 34654 / (727) 868-8657 / info@pubprof.com

Treasure Chest

Programs & books to help you Reach *Your* Stars!

PROGRAMS *to help you reach your stars!*

Reach Your Stars!™ by Debbie Happy Cohen
A seminar for people of all ages to discover their dreams,overcome their obstacles and reach their stars! (813) 931-7707

Redirect Your Life by Cindy Kocher and Mel Fergenbaum
A life-changing weekend course for adults. Teen course is available too! (727) 596-3653

The Silva Method by José Silva
A 2 *weekend course. The principles of this course will help you to use more of your brain to work smarter, not harder. Great for teens and up.* (800) 545-6463

Redirecting Children's Behavior by Katherine Kvols
This class is for everyone! The techniques work with children, adults, and pets too! Call 1-800-257-9002 *for information and courses in your area.*

REFERENCES

OVERALL EXCELLENCE

Chicken Soup for the Soul series by Jack Canfield and Mark Victor Hansen
Excuse Me, Your Life is Waiting by Lynn Grabhorn
How to Win Friends and Influence People by Dale Carnegie
The Artist's Way by Julia Cameron
The Learning Revolution by Gordon Dryden and Jeannette Vos
The Silva Method by José Silva

FINANCES

Rich Dad, Poor Dad by Robert T. Kiyosaki with Sharon Lechter
The Richest Man in Babylon by George Carson
Think and Grow Rich by Napoleon Hill

TIME MANAGEMENT

First Things First
The 7 Habits of Highly Effective Families
The 7 Habits of Highly Effective People
all by Stephen R. Covey

HEALTH

Ageless Body, Timeless Mind by Deepak Choprah, M.D.
Fit for Life by Harvey and Marilyn Diamond
Healing Back Pain by John Sarno, M.D.
Love, Medicine and Miracles by Bernie Siegel, M.D.

RELATIONSHIPS & LOVE

Life Strategies by Phil McGraw
Life Strategies for Teens by Jay McGraw
Love Is Letting Go of Fear by Gerald G. Jampolsky, M.D.
The Bridge Across Forever by Richard Bach

FRIENDSHIPS

All books by SARK
All books by Leo Buscaglia, especially **Living, Loving and Learning**

PARENTING

Redirecting Children's Behavior by Kathryn Kvols
STEP: Systematic Training for Effective Parenting
by Don Dinkmeyer, Ph.D. & Don Dinkmeyer, Jr., Ph.D.

CAREER

I Could Do Anything If I Only Knew What It Was by Barbara Sher
The Artist's Way at Work by Mark Bryan with Julia Cameron and Catherine Allen
What Color Is Your Parachute? by Richard Nelson Bolles
All books by Ken Blanchard & Dr. Spencer Johnson, M.D.

COMMUNITY ACTION

The Earth Charter visit www.earthcharter.org / www earthchartersummits.org (see page 134)

Activities for Classrooms and Dream Teams

The following group activities promote self-discovery, appreciation of others and strength-building. Most can be easily tailored to all grade levels. It is a good idea to play inspiring music in the background to create a mood conducive to creativity and exploration.

★ **Paper Plate of Passions**

Each student has a paper plate and crayons or markers. The student draws at least five dreams that he or she has (places to visit, people to know, things to do).

★ **Values Deck**

Have the class create a deck of cards of the class' most important values. Each student chooses a different value and writes their value on one side and a symbolic picture on the other. Cards are shuffled weekly and students are grouped into threesomes. Each group receives three cards and makes up a story to promote and encourage those values.

★ **101 list**

Each student writes 101 things they want to accomplish in their lifetime. This might take a few hours, but it is well worth it.

★ **What Do You Really Want?**

If they are old enough, students are asked at the beginning of the school year (or before Thanksgiving) to answer the question: "What do you want?" The day they turn in the paper, they are then asked to write: "What do you really want?" (i.e. Why do you want those other things? What will they give you? Power, joy, love. .?) This paper can be collected and given back to the students at the end of the year.

★ **Lucky Logo**

Each student draws a "logo" or symbol that represents their best self. Bring in pictures of different logos to give them examples. Hang up their logo with their baby photo next to it.

★ **The Most Precious Page**

Each child writes the names of everyone in their class and something kind about each person. The papers are collected and an adult compiles a list for each student of what their classmates wrote. The student receives the page describing all of the encouraging and kind words.

★ **You Are Make A Difference**

Purchase ribbons or create certificates for each child. Call each child up to the front of the class and tell him or her why they make a difference. Give each child extra ribbons to give to other people make a difference to them. Ask the children to come back with their stories.

★ **Putting "Can'ts" to Rest**

Students write reasons why they can't achieve their dreams and goals on small slips of paper. They are placed in a box and a buried in the ground. For effect, a funeral can be held.

★ **Loving and Listening**

Students sit in pairs, back to back. Each student listens for 5 minutes while the other one speaks. The second person is not allowed to comment on what the other person said, he or she just listens. Sitting back to back helps eliminate the desire for verbal conversation or retaliation.

★ **Redirect Bullies**

Bring out the outstanding leader within a bully. The next time a student gets into trouble for bullying, have him or her read to someone else who reads worse than he does. Help him or her channel negative energy into positive activity where his or her strengths can be used to serve.

★ **Success Story Teller**

One child a week tells a story to the rest of the class of how someone accomplished a dream. It could be about themselves, or about a hero of theirs.

★ **Attendance List of Dreamers**

Write each student's dream next to their name and imagine them reaching their stars every time you call their name for attendance!

★ **A Giving Tree**

Draw a tree with your favorite fruits. Have others write the strengths they see in you on each fruit of your tree.

★ **Thank Your Mentor**

Each person writes a thank you letter to their mentor or someone who has inspired them, describing how they have been touched and how their lives have been changed.

★ **Teach Tolerance**

Invite speakers to share their challenges and how they have overcome them or now live with them successfully. Examples: physical disability, drug addiction, etc. Read stories that express the real feelings of people who have been oppressed like The Diary of Anne Frank. Have the group journal and discuss their raw feelings.

Do you have good ideas? Share your ideas at ***www.reachyourstars.com*** and we'll create an idea garden.

Add your own ideas here:

___

___

___

___

___

___

___

57 Ways to Awaken a Creative Genius

These steps are truly simple and require only a willingness and a desire for a better way. They work!

1. Give someone a compliment.
2. Say something kind about someone else behind their back.
3. Listen without interrupting for 5 minutes.
4. Join a program in your school.
5. Cut out all complaining.
6. Bake cookies for a close friend.
7. Leave someone a message on their answering machine telling them that they are awesome!
8. Write a thank you note to someone who has been a mentor to you.
9. Write one kind thing about everyone in your class.
10. Have a dream and share your dream with someone.
11. Mentor someone younger than you, or mentor someone older than you.
12. Draw a fruit tree. Write a strength of yours on each fruit.
13. Give and receive a hug at least once a day.
14. Do something to make someone else smile or laugh.
15. Take 5 minutes to breathe deeply today; relax. Imitate your cat, dog or pet.
16. Think of 5 things that you are grateful for.
17. First thing in the morning, decide what kind of day you want to have today.
18. Give yourself a self high five for something you did right.
19. Write 5 things that you did right today (Tied your shoes? That counts!)
20. Imagine a peaceful world.
21. Notice one person in school who seems shy and unnoticed.
22. Read a story out loud to someone you love (Chicken Soup for the Soul has great ones!)
23. Tell someone else a story of something foolish that you did . . . it will make them feel less stupid and more human, too.
24. Decide to do one thing different today (i.e. brush your teeth with your opposite hand).
25. Write all of your "I Can't's", put them in a box, and bury them.
26. Give a smile to someone today.
27. Take your mentor out to lunch and thank him or her.
28. When someone "makes" you angry, choose a different response.
29. Draw a scribble drawing portrait of your best friend.

30. Take a moment of silence before you begin each day.
31. Become friends with your books.
32. Create a Success Team of 3 or more people. Hold each other accountable to your dreams. Celebrate your baby steps!
33. Play "feelings" charades to expand your emotional vocabulary.
34. Tell someone you love him or her.
35. Write a poem and read it out loud.
36. Spend one hour by yourself doing something fun – just for you.
37. Ask your friends what their dreams are – what success, happiness and love means to them.
38. Listen to all the sounds around you for 5 minutes.
39. Ask someone to tell you what they are most proud of.
40. Start a journal.
41. Send a dollar to a Realistic Dreamer, with a note that tells them that the dollar represents your support of their dream.
42. Say hello today to someone you've never noticed before.
43. Make four new friends this year.
44. The next time you want to complain, Stop. Focus on a solution or stay quiet.
45. Send a thank you note to a parent, child, or teacher. Tell that person what they did specifically that you appreciate.
46. Focus on Progress and on Effort.
47. Listen to a song that lifts you HIGH!
48. Make a tape of inspiring songs and give it to your friends.
49. Spend a moment in silence before your next exam – give thanks for your ability to take the test.
50. Ask that whatever happens, it is for the highest good for all.
51. Identify a routine behavior (i.e., the order you put your clothes on) and do it differently.
52. Either sitting or lying down, with eyes closed, walk through an exotic land.
53. Tell a friend 3 things you would love to do with them before the end of the year.
54. Next time you encounter a problem, brainstorm until you find 3 solutions.
55. Go on a nature walk and observe without speaking.
56. Lay on your back outdoors, and watch the clouds float by.
57. Read a book upside down, and smile!

Reach Your Stars!™ Seminar Outline

45-minute Seminar outline for Kids and Adults

Reach Your Stars! seminars include participants of all ages, but tailor as needed, according to age.

Once you have read this book and completed the exercises in it, you may want to present the following _Reach Your Stars!_ seminar to your class. Besides being fun, it boosts morale and motivatic while allowing participants to discover their dreams and reach for their stars! It works best when your audience is cheering, laughing and crying. Get their emotions involved by including heartful and funny stories!

1. Who are the fastest learners in the human race? Children.
Why? They are curious, they ask questions (lots), they are playful and they are not afraid to make mistakes. Be like a child and you will get the most out of this seminar.

2. Meet and greet your partner. Share something fun about yourself.

3. Each participant draws a stick figure "dream maker™" including:

- Stars in the sky (representing dreams)
- A light bulb (representing ideas)
- A smile (representing positive attitude)
- A big heart (representing kindness)
- Eyes looking up at the stars (representing vision)
- Ears (representing listening and observing)
- One hand reaching up and forward (for the stars)
- One hand reaching behind (to help others)
- Feet moving forward on a path

This drawing will reinforce the concepts kinesthetically and visually provide future reference for the seminar's primary objectives.

Write the answers to the following questions:

a. _Who do you consider to be a creative genius?_ Write their names next to the light bulb and be sure to remind them to include people from different cultures or nationalities.
b. _What are your dreams?_ Write your dreams next to the stars on the drawing.
c. _Whom do you appreciate or love?_ Write their name next to the heart on the drawing.

4. Review the YES formula for building positive healthy relationships with yourself & others. (Refer to the introduction of this book for an overview.)

You are wonderful and beautiful; you were born that way!
Everyone else is unique, special and wonderful too!
Start sharing appreciation today.

Read "_Who You Are Makes a Difference_" by Helice Bridges written in _Chicken Soup for the Soul_ - _first boo_ (for more mature children). Participants pair up and share something special about their partner.

5. Review the **I AM** formula for making dreams come true. (Refer to the introduction of this book for an overview).

> ***Imagination:*** Chapters 2 & 3. You can use what smart advertisers know about how your mind works to change your own behavior - chapter 3.
> ***Attitude:*** Chapters 4 & 5. Know that you can reach your dreams, like a child reaching for a cookie on a counter.
> ***Motion:*** Chapters 6 & 7. Identify baby steps you can take and focus on the positive; see the example of dolphins learning to "fly" – chapter 4.

6. Apply the formulas by taking action:

- Write the name of someone you will thank for making a difference and what you will do to thank them (write it next to the hand reaching out).
- State one small step you will take toward your dream (write it next to the feet).

7. **YES, I AM!** Ask a question and state the response with the group:

What does the **Y** stand for?	YOU!
What does the **E** stand for?	EVERYONE ELSE!
What does the **S** stand for?	START NOW!
What does the **I** stand for?	IMAGINATION!
What does the **A** stand for?	ATTITUDE!
What does the **M** stand for?	MOTION!

8. Make a commitment to your partner and tell them the actions you wrote in step six.

9. Thank your partner sincerely using eye contact.

10. Reinforce the **YES I AM!** formulas by asking questions out loud and have the audience answer "YES I AM!" in unison.

• Are you going to reach for your dreams?	"YES I AM!"
• Are you awesome?	"YES I AM!"
• Are you going to show appreciation to others?	"YES I AM!"
• Include any concept you want to reinforce.	"YES I AM!"

For longer seminars, include more experiential techniques. Refer to Group Activities on page 159 and the next page.

YES:

You And Everyone else: Strength Tree. Draw a tree with your favorite fruits. Have others write the strengths they see in you on each fruit of your tree.
Start sharing: Hand out ribbons that say YES I AM! Reaching For The Stars!

I AM:

Imagination: Teach how relaxation and visualization are used by professional athletes to improve their game and by students to improve their grades. Explain how clowns are taught to relax their bodies by imagining themselves as limp old socks so they can fall down easily and use their energy more effectively.
Attitude: Write a list of weaknesses and the strengths each weakness offers.
Motion: Copy the Weekly Success Habits sheet and have participants write their action steps on it and make a commitment to use the sheet for at least 7 days.

Glossary

Attention
Attention is the act of giving time to something, like "baby steps" on the way to success. It is feeding a baby in the middle of the night. It is five minutes of writing in your book whenever there is time. Consistent attention creates change.

Attitude
Is the only REAL choice you have about anything. Everything else follows: your thoughts, your words, your behavior, your relationships. An attitude consciously focused on GRATITUDE is the foundation of a joyful and successful life.

Dream or Vision
Vision is what you see when you look within and are in the process of creating something. Vision gives you guidance about where to go, what to do, and how to get there. Vision is a exercise for accessing your intuition. It also offers a wonderful way to create the life you most desire by first deciding who you want to be and who you want to become. Vision comes from the heart. Looking within to define yourself is the only TRUE path.

Focus
Focus is where you place your attention. (i.e., don't think of the color red.)
What you focus your attention on will grow. You choose what to focus on.

Goals
The necessary steps to make a dream come true.

Gratitude
This is the only attitude that makes sense regarding *everything* in life. It brings sanity, peace, joy and contentment. Gratitude means you know there is a gift for you in all of life's circumstances and, that you are willing to project your attention there to experience and enjoy.

Intention
Your intention is the REAL thought behind all of your facades. The way to know what your REAL intention is, very simple. Watch your feet. What does your behavior show? Examine your feelings. Do they resonate with your behaviors (congruence), or do your feet go one way while your mind goes another (guilt)? Intention is what moves people to act the way they do. There is no wrong or right on this level. Intention is the most powerful force I know of when it is followed by attention.

Intuition
Intuition is your inner sense of knowingness about where you need to be and when. It is a gut feeling, a heartfelt sense, a small voice, a message from a stranger. You know the message to be true because of this inner feeling. A feeling that says "yes." It guides you based on your intent and your vision.

Magnetism
Your thoughts and feelings, which are backed up by intention and attention, act as a magnet, unconsciously. It is up to you to decide where to place your focus. Your mind works in images. If you know what you don't want, you'll get that because you'll picture it and feel it. For example: not wanting to be fat is much different than choosing health, vibrancy, vitality, and fitness.

Questions
Your life questions are your guides. They tell you more about where you are going than any of you answers do. Your life mysteries guide you to the answers you seek. They guide your attention to people and places that await you with gifts.

Relationships
Relationships are our wonderful opportunity to experience and become who we choose to be. They are our mirrors. People who make life changes also find themselves letting go of old relationships and building new ones. People that push your buttons the most are your greatest teachers, because they can only push your buttons if you have buttons to be pushed! You can only see in another what you are capable of believing about yourself.

Self
The self is our unique individuality and how each one of us fits into the world. Before everything else, we must care for the self; physically, mentally, spiritually, emotionally and socially. If we are not taken care of, it is difficult to care for others and to maintain balance. In an airplane, passengers are warned that in case of an emergency, adults should put on their life masks first, before putting one on their children. Take care of your self so that you can live fully!

A Message for Every Child

You are loved, lovable, and loving.
You are divine.
You are here to discover your unique talent
and expression in this world and to cultivate it.
When you do this, true success will come easily to you.
You will not only attract wealth, but you will feel excited
about living and you will know that you have a place
in the world. There is something that you can do
better than anyone else in the whole world.
Discover this and share it.
Meditate. Learn to silence your mind,
for in that silence, you are open to guidance
from the highest part of yourself.
From this place, you will never doubt who you are or
what you need to do.
Appreciate all that you have and all that you are.
Count your blessings every day.
What you focus your attention on grows stronger.
Give something to everyone you meet – a smile,
a silent prayer, a flower, a hug, a note, money,
a book, words of encouragement or appreciation.
You realize how much you have only
when you give it away.
Make up your own rules. Live the life that you want.
Be creative and never be afraid to take risks.
You are the artist of your life.
Beautify it with all that brings you joy.
There are no failures, only lessons.
Learn from your mistakes and don't be afraid
to make them. You only become stronger when
you get back up. And you can only fall forward.
Persistence pays off, so keep moving
in the direction you want to go.
You are never alone. You are always divinely guided,
protected, and loved.

At the End of Each Day

At the end of each day, this is how I like to feel . . .

Grateful for all that I am and satisfied with all that I have;
A sense of knowing that I am totally secure;
At peace, having let go of all that is not loving and good;
Like a queen, I am taken care of . . . I have given a lot
and I am receiving even more;
Content, assured that I am exactly where I need to be;
Relaxed and healthy, my mind's peace
reflecting in my body;
Like a child – as though God is holding me
in the palm of his hand, sharing His love,
His light, His joy with me, filling me with warmth;
I feel safe and I sleep like a baby.

About the Author

Debbie Happy Cohen

"Is that really your middle name?" Debbie gets asked this question by almost everyone she meets. "Happy" comes from being proudly named after her great-grandmother, Simcha, a heroine of her time. In Hebrew, the word "simcha" means "happy" and her mother translated the name literally for Debbie's middle name.

Debbie Happy Cohen is a first-generation American-born Iraqi Jew, and she knows the value of living the American dream. After years of personal research and observation, Debbie discovered a golden thread of truth that is found in every story of achievement in the world – including yours. Her "I Am" formula for success will empower you to dream big – but realistically – to make your dreams come true NOW. This formula is easy to remember and apply, and is taught to people of all ages.

Debbie has mentored children for over 14 years, coached thousands of people for over 10 years, and her biggest dream is coming true right now – *you* reading this book and reaching *your* stars. Debbie is the owner and president of Total Success Coaching, Inc. Her formal education includes a Bachelor's degree in Psychology and a Master's Degree in Counselor Education.

Debbie's personal favorite successes:

- ★ One teenager building a community outreach program in his school, immediately following a *Reach Your Stars!* seminar.
- ★ A physical therapist quadrupling her business in four months.
- ★ An entire classroom of middle school students remembering the 'I AM' formula three months after a 10-minute speech.
- ★ One elementary school raising $12,000 in seven months to enhance their media center by developing stronger community partnerships.

"Take a dream and make it real and share it with the world. Because if that dream can affect another's soul, then how many more dreams would you make come true?"

Jeremy Valdes, *age* 15

Services Available:

Debbie Happy Cohen speaks to schools, conventions, and organizations. Her messages are available on CD and video. In addition, Total Success Coaching, Inc. conducts seminars and in-depth coaching for individuals, school leaders, businesses and associations. A complete list of seminars is listed on page vii at the beginning of this book.

Debbie wants to hear from you! Submit success stories, testimonials, challenges & questions, or find out about Debbie's current activities and programs by contacting:

(813) 931-7707 • Fax: (813) 354-3540
www.reachyourstars.com

"Wall of Dreams"

Debbie's "Wall of Dreams" is a positive symbol for the future of our world. Her goal is to collect one million dreams from people all over the United States and share them in her seminars as a backdrop and a symbol of unity among the people of the nation. If you would like to include your dream, write it down in this box, cut it out and send it to the address at the bottom of the page.

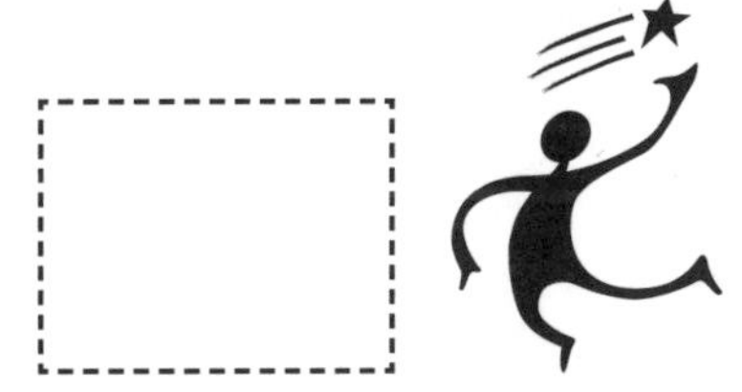

Classrooms:

Children of all ages who know how to write (or can have someone write for them) can do this!

Teachers can duplicate the same box shown (we suggest purchasing labels of the same size (easier for them to write on), adhere them to an 8 1/2 x 11 piece of paper and send to the same address below. Be sure to include the following information: Teacher's name, grade level, number of students in your class, school's name, phone number and address. Mail 8 1/2 x 11 dream sheets" to:

Debbie Happy Cohen • PO Box 0486, Miami, FL 33163